IT'S ALL PERSONAL

*12 Lessons Learned Through
Cancer Survival That Transformed
My Career Success*

KEVIN A. JANSEN

ENDORSEMENTS

"Kevin weaves his fight with leukemia with his professional and personal experiences to create a compelling case for living life – personally and professionally – purposefully and passionately. His twelve lessons learned are poignant reminders for each of us to prioritize our relationships and cultivate them through commitment, honesty and trust, with genuine respect for others and ourselves."

—**Mark Williamson,**
Partner at Lathrop GPM

"One man's profoundly bad luck is eclipsed by his extreme lifestyle choice to overcome at all costs. His aim was to not just survive cancer, but to thrive in its wake. This compelling story is for anyone that has questioned fate, gratitude and the reason for living. This is a MUST read!"

—**Melissa Albers,**
Owner of The Authentic Leader

"An incredible story about the journey and challenges that go with a man's battle with leukemia. The lessons learned and shared by Kevin are profound. If you want perspective on life, the good and bad, you will find it with this story."

—**Kurt Rakos,**
Co-Founder and Partner at SkyWater Search Partners

IT'S ALL PERSONAL

*12 Lessons Learned Through
Cancer Survival That Transformed
My Career Success*

KEVIN A. JANSEN

It's All Personal: 12 Lessons Learned Through Cancer Survival That Transformed My Career Success

Copyright © 2023 by Kevin A. Jansen

All rights reserved. No part of this publication may be reproduced, distributed, or transmitted in any form or by any means, including photocopying, recording, or other electronic or mechanical methods, without the prior written permission of the author, except in the case of brief quotations embodied in critical reviews and certain other noncommercial uses permitted by copyright law.

Jones Media Publishing
10645 N. Tatum Blvd. Ste. 200-166
Phoenix, AZ 85028
www.JonesMediaPublishing.com

Disclaimer:

The author strives to be as accurate and complete as possible in the creation of this book, notwithstanding the fact that the author does not warrant or represent at any time that the contents within are accurate due to the rapidly changing nature of the Internet.

While all attempts have been made to verify information provided in this publication, the Author and the Publisher assume no responsibility and are not liable for errors, omissions, or contrary interpretation of the subject matter herein. The Author and Publisher hereby disclaim any liability, loss or damage incurred as a result of the application and utilization, whether directly or indirectly, of any information, suggestion, advice, or procedure in this book. Any perceived slights of specific persons, peoples, or organizations are unintentional.

In practical advice books, like anything else in life, there are no guarantees of income made. Readers are cautioned to rely on their own judgment about their individual circumstances to act accordingly. Readers are responsible for their own actions, choices, and results. This book is not intended for use as a source of legal, business, accounting or financial advice. All readers are advised to seek the services of competent professionals in legal, business, accounting, and finance field.

Printed in the United States of America
ISBN: 978-1-948382-52-6 paperback

DEDICATION

To the doctors, nurses, and medical staff that helped me to survive. Without you, I would have never seen my children become awe inspiring adults.

ACKNOWLEDGEMENTS

I would like to thank my wife Gretchen for consistently supporting me in my effort to make this idea a reality. She truly is my trusted partner and soulmate.

From the day they were each born, my kids have been the center of my life. They provided me with the inspiration to choose to fight rather than give up when I was first diagnosed with leukemia. Without them, I would not be here today.

I would like to thank Beth for adding color to my stories in the early phases of my writing. I may have given up on myself if she hadn't encouraged me to keep going.

I would like to thank my first wife Christina for taking care of our kids almost exclusively alone while I was fighting to survive. Our kids wouldn't be who they are today without you.

And last but not least, I want to thank Justine. Your emails and phone calls were invaluable.

TABLE OF CONTENTS

Introduction 1

Chapter 1: An Unexpected Problem 3

Chapter 2: Trust and Integrity............................ 9

Chapter 3: Personalized Problem Solving 17

Chapter 4: Authentic Differentiation 25

Chapter 5: Success Is a Choice 33

Chapter 6: It Takes a Team 41

Chapter 7: The Cancer of Infighting 49

Chapter 8: Proactively Invest in Relationships 57

Chapter 9: Moral Compass Over Money 67

Chapter 10: Perseverance Prevails 75

Chapter 11: Win/Win or Win/Lose....................... 85

Chapter 12: Breakups Are Part of Life 93

Chapter 13: Urgency vs Regret 101

Chapter 14: Conclusion 109

About Kevin Jansen 111

INTRODUCTION

Do you find yourself getting up each morning and wondering why you are going to work each day? Are you careening through your daily routine thinking that someday, you will find more happiness at work, home, or both? If that is the case, then let this book serve as your wake-up call to confidently, and urgently, change course to a more successful and meaningful life.

The contents of this book will depict how you can turn something as unthinkable as a diagnosis with a life-threatening disease into a life-altering gift through teamwork and perseverance. It will provide you with a guide for how to develop, assess, and manage more productive business and personal relationships, which will enable you to achieve greater success at work and at home. It will also serve as a powerful reminder to act with fearless urgency today as complacency and indecision will lead to regret and an unfulfilled life tomorrow.

My diagnosis snatched my career away from me and put a hole in my retirement savings. It took away my friends, ended my marriage, and cost me several of the most productive years of my life. It also put my three children through hell. The road to rebuild what I had lost seemed endless.

What I learned along that road made it all worth it.

In each chapter you will find anecdotes about the physical and emotional pain that cancer bestowed on me, and the great people who helped me survive against the odds. You will also read short stories about my triumphs, and missteps, in my career. The most important message being that the core pillars of success at home and in the office are the same: relationships, teamwork, and trust.

CHAPTER 1

AN UNEXPECTED PROBLEM

The Day Cancer and I First Met

Late one afternoon, I found myself in an office with a man who had introduced himself to me only three days earlier. My entire lower back and pelvis ached, and my brain was numb from the IV infused Demerol that had been given to me an hour earlier.

I had to move some books off a chair in his cluttered office to sit down. Then I heard the unimaginable news. "I am glad I caught you before your wife arrived to pick you up. Your preliminary bone marrow biopsy results show that you have leukemia."

My mind shot back to the online research my wife and I had done the night before. We had learned that leukemia had two distinct subtypes, acute and chronic. And that the 5-year survival rate for acute leukemia was 15%, and that chronic leukemia was a much better alternative.

I was terrified, but I anxiously interrupted him mid-sentence. "Is it acute or chronic?"

The oncologist responded, "Acute. I don't know the specific type that you have yet, but it's treatable."

After the word "treatable," my mind shut down. I was stuck on the word "treatable" as it sounded horribly different than "curable."

With the oncologist's help, I made a follow-up appointment for the next afternoon, and I proceeded to walk through the long, sterile halls of the hospital in disbelief. I made my way to the entrance, spotted my wife and kids, and I climbed into the passenger seat of our minivan. Christina knew something was wrong as soon as I sat down. I told her. We made the entire 35-minute drive home in silence, trying to hold ourselves together. At the same time, our kids laughed, bickered, and fought like all siblings do in their car seats behind us.

I didn't want to be in the minivan, and I didn't want to go home. I wasn't sure I wanted to live through the physical and emotional torture that would soon follow either.

Trauma Transformed to A Gift

From an outsider's perspective, my life at the time looked perfect. My wife of 10 years, Christina, and I owned a recently built 3,500 sq./ft. home with a small mortgage on 2.5 acres of land 20 miles outside of the Twin Cities in Minnesota. On the day I was diagnosed, we had three happy and healthy young children, and the five of us had all the material possessions that we wanted or needed.

Before getting married, Christina and I avidly pursued our shared passion for travel. We backpacked through Europe for almost four months, starting in London, ending in the Greek Isles, and stopping in many countries in between. For our honeymoon, we spent two weeks exploring Bali, Bangkok, Singapore and Hong Kong. We returned to Europe two more times before the inevitable constraints of a family set in. We were pretty sure our first child was conceived in London, and once we confirmed the news, we planned one last fling to Hawaii. We were the definition of young and free.

When I learned I had cancer, our oldest son, Vincent, was 6 years old. I could already tell he was going to be a perfectionist and focused on family, as he openly loved his mom, dad, and sisters. His grandfather was drafted by the Chicago Cubs, and when I saw him pick up a golf club for the first time, I instantly knew where his natural swing came from.

Olivia was 4 years old, and she proudly wore a pink T-shirt that proclaimed her to be "Daddy's Girl" on the front of it. I vividly remember picking her up in my arms and dancing around the living room with Smash Mouth blaring in the background when she was a toddler. She was destined to be a gymnast from the day she crawled out of her crib, crashed on the floor headfirst, and came out of her bedroom beaming like she had just scored a perfect 10.

Isabel, 2 years old, was the last one to arrive. She didn't have a T-shirt that announced her connection to her mom, but she was never far away from Christina. On the outside, she was reserved. But I could tell there was something inside of her waiting to break out. Before reaching her teens, I learned what it was when out of the blue she confidently proclaimed to me, "I am not going to be like Vincent and Olivia." She was her own person then and she still is today.

My career had followed an equally adventurous path as my travels, marriage, and family life. Before the age of 30, I had climbed the org chart at a publicly traded regional brokerage firm with ease. After starting as an entry level analyst, four years later I was co-managing more than $1 billion of real estate loans and securities.

During the last 2 years in my position, I was charged with developing working relationships with the most prominent investment banks on Wall Street to efficiently liquidate more than $2 billion of complex securities. That work led me to appear before the Board of Directors of the company quarterly as the viability of its ongoing business was somewhat dependent on my work. My compensation tracked the rapid rise in my responsibilities.

Recognizing that I was frustrated with the pace at which my firm was addressing some significant challenges, an early mentor of mine pulled me aside and said, "You need to step back and have kids or something. You already know everything about investments and the brokerage business. Now you need to be patient and gain some experience." I knew he was right, yet I was also young and impatient to a fault. I ultimately left my job as moving on seemed more attractive than waiting.

Over the next 5 years, I started a business in partnership with my brother, and I acquired a minority interest in two other businesses. Through that experience I grew to love working with small companies and the energy of entrepreneurs. I still have that passion today. At the time of my diagnosis, I was 37 years old and working as the leader of the Corporate Finance Department at a closely held brokerage firm.

On a Friday in late July, I physically felt a little bit off. On Tuesday of the following week, I learned I had acute myeloid leukemia (AML), one of the most fatal and rapidly moving types of cancer. By Thursday morning, I had checked into the hospital with an uncertain release date. Without immediate treatment, I would have died a week or two later. The pace at which my life changed was breathtaking, even by my standards.

Ironically, I immediately knew that I was facing much more than a cancer diagnosis.

My Relationship with Cancer

Cancer has been a partner in my life for as long as I can remember. That partnership started when I was only 14 months old when my mom died of breast cancer in her early 30's. I am not sure I will ever fully recover from that painful loss. Several years later, and just a couple of years prior to my diagnosis, my dad died of lung cancer. He was in his mid-60's. My own relationship with the disease became part of what I have come to appreciate as my continuous learning experience with cancers' life-altering challenges.

While attending my dads' funeral, comments shared with me by a number of the attendees had a lasting impact on me. Given his young age and visibility in the local community, hundreds of people attended his service. None of them mentioned to me the fact that he had accumulated a significant amount of wealth during his career. None of them talked about the spectacular home he had built on one of the Twin Cities premier lakes or the retirement home he owned in Florida. They all went out of their way to tell me that he was a great man and friend.

For some people, success is defined by how much money they can accumulate during their career. For others, their success is defined by a great marriage or raising happy and well-adjusted adult children. And there are also people who devote their lives to finding meaning and purpose through their religious beliefs, dedication to non-profit causes, or other endeavors. Cancer taught me lessons that I have come to rely on to achieve success in all those things.

CHAPTER 2

TRUST AND INTEGRITY

*Let a Child's Pure Perspective
Guide You As an Adult*

After my initial diagnosis, a whirlwind of activity came to pass: Telling friends. Telling relatives. Getting my life in order for what I was told was – in the best case – a series of hospital stays.

Or worst case: The possibility I may never check out of the hospital.

I focused on the best of all best cases: four to six weeks in the hospital, followed by a short release to recuperate at home before doing it all over again. In all likelihood, I was facing five rounds of chemotherapy which, if successful, would end my nightmare. My oncologist had explained to me that given my young age I had a 40% chance of survival. Not great, but better odds than the 15% I had found online.

The hardest thing that I faced in dealing with my new diagnosis was how to tell my three kids. Christina and I firmly believed that kids were best served with honesty. Sometimes that honesty needed to be modified, but honesty, nonetheless.

We called them together and had them sit down on the stairway going upstairs. We did the best we could to explain that their dad was very sick, and that he needed to go into the hospital for a very long time. As 2-, 4-, and 6-year olds, they needed the news delivered in a very simple manner. It was like a dream, maybe more like a nightmare, saying the words. And both Christina and I had a very difficult time telling the story without having a complete breakdown.

I knew that I was changing my children's lives forever. I figured that the moment would be etched in their memory, and I could not bear that thought. I also could not bear the thought that they could be left without a father. It was one of the hardest two minutes of my life. The conversation ended with "Do you have any questions?" To which they said, "No."

I felt horrible that they didn't and probably couldn't fully understand. At the same time, I was happy for their naïve approach to life. I was sick. I was going into the hospital. They could not understand how life would be different.

That evening as I tried to unwind from the day's events, I went outside and stood by the swing set watching my son Vince. He slowly drifted back and forth in the swing, getting some simple comfort from the steady rhythm and early August fresh air. I just wanted to be near him, and I could tell he was thinking about something. Then it finally came out.

"If you die, will Mom find another dad for us?" He kept his steady back and forth sway while asking the most emotionally powerful question that I have ever had to answer.

My eyes started to fill with water as my mind raced to choose my words. I was not sure I could speak much less answer his question. Finally, I said, "If I die, I sure hope Mom finds another dad for you and the girls. We are not there yet though, so let's hope that I will be your dad for a long time to come." He just kept swinging without interruption.

As an adult, my life was so complicated. It was filled with responsibilities and worries. For my 6-year-old son, it was so clear, so pure, and uncomplicated. Who will I love if it isn't you, Dad? Who will take care of me? Who will play baseball and golf with me when I am older? I look back today at his question, and I am awed by how unburdened his life was and how simple my life should be. Who will I love? Who will take care of me? Who will I share life's successes and challenges with?

Ironically, these core human needs and desires are the same for a young child and for an adult. I believe that on some level each of us already knows that. But it wasn't until that day that I was able to embrace it.

Relationships, Trust, Honesty

It is human nature to make life a lot more complicated than it needs to be. That is particularly true as we get older. Children are blessed with an ability to cut to what really matters, while adults can overanalyze and worry about things that many times are less important or meaningless. That is particularly true when faced with ethical challenges or issues where personal trust is called into question. The emotional baggage that we pick up on our path to becoming adults can complicate what should be easy.

My experience with cancer led me to have a heightened awareness of all that really matters in life. And yes, it's simple. Our lives and our legacy are defined by our relationships and the trust and honesty we invest in developing and maintaining them. Without trust and honesty, our relationships often become unproductive, strained, or in some cases toxic, which eventually bleeds into our entire lives.

Relying on this deeper understanding, I can predict with frightening accuracy the ripple effects of a poor decision, especially one that calls into question trust and honesty. Whether it be in our personal lives, or in the office, complex problems that require solutions often land in a long loop of indecision and second guessing of priorities. Yet many times, the answer is right in front of us, hidden behind our own best judgment, meaningless concerns, or fear.

The Price of Dishonesty

Early in my career I was presented with the opportunity to purchase $8 million of loans on residential houses that were constructed in a rural development outside of Charlotte. At the time, I was managing $1 billion of real estate assets for a money management firm, and while $8 million was a big investment, in the scope of my role and responsibilities at the time, it was relatively small.

The broker representing the seller of the loans, I will refer to her as Melinda, first came to me through a cold call. That fact alone led me to approach the opportunity with a fair amount of skepticism. Melinda was a smart, engaging woman, but there was something about her that put my guard up. Initially, everything on paper added up. But at that stage of my career, there were other less tangible signs that I was inclined to overlook, ignore, or I missed altogether.

She didn't seem to be consistently forthcoming with key pieces of information, and there was a little bit too much "sales shine" on everything that she shared with me. Over the course of a handful of weeks conducting my due diligence, I could feel my trust waning rather than building. I considered walking away from the opportunity, but after a discussion with my co-fund manager, we decided that neither one of us saw anything that justified dropping from the deal.

I moved forward and took numerous steps to protect our investment while looking over my shoulder financially and legally at every turn. After making what should have been a simple transaction incredibly complicated, the deal closed. Over time, our fund earned an attractive financial return with the risk mitigating guardrails that I put in place. That was the good news.

Now for the bad news. In the months and years following closing, we heard numerous complaints from the homeowners about poor construction quality. The houses were the ultimate security for our loans and investment, so that caused me some sleepless nights.

To give you a sense of how bad it was, to save construction costs, a handful of the homes were built without septic systems, and sewage was being pumped underground, directly into the homes' backyards. Enforcing loan repayment from homeowners whose kids could no longer play in their backyard was not a fun experience. Yet, on behalf of our investors, we legally had to.

In retrospect, I wish I had known then what I do now. Today, I am not only skeptical of a cold call, I won't take a cold call at all. On the rare occasion a blind sales call gets through to me, I tell the salesperson to do some research and find someone that we have a common business connection with. Then have that person refer the salesperson to me. That way, the introduction comes through a trusted business relationship.

I would also never proceed to a closing today based on information that seems sketchy or incomplete. I have learned that smart people who are not completely upfront and honest will find a way to get something over on me. Dishonest people survive in business by being skilled at their craft of dishonesty, and while steps can be taken to try and protect yourself, you will ultimately come out on the short end of things.

Over the 24 months post-closing of our deal, there were numerous lawsuits filed against the real estate developer. I should not have been surprised to hear that this developer was very comfortable in a courtroom as he had a long history of legal troubles. If I had only done some deeper due diligence upfront on the seller himself, I would have discovered the pending lawsuits and the long list of unhappy people chasing behind him. Those obvious red flags would have saved our team a considerable amount of time and distress.

Tying It Together

The foundation of any personal or professional relationship is trust. Without trust, you have very little to work with in terms of developing and maintaining a relationship. Not to mention the likelihood of getting taken advantage of rises dramatically. If a client tells me without cause that they need a lower price every time we do business together, I can no longer trust them to be upfront with me. If an employee consistently asks for a raise without a well thought out justification as to why, the manager/employee relationship is tarnished.

But trust is impossible to earn or keep without honesty. When the truth is hidden, trust is second guessed and doubted until the relationship is tarnished or falls apart altogether.

I strive for 100% honesty in everything that I do in the office. Is it practical to share every thought, opinion, or fact with everyone, always? No. But is there ever an excuse for intentionally misleading someone? No. There are times when information needs to be withheld. But as soon as the need to withhold information passes, I know I'm obligated to go back to my relationship and openly explain my actions and decisions.

In the middle of a crisis, my son was most concerned with whether he would continue to have a relationship with someone that he could implicitly trust and depend on to help him navigate life's challenges. My wife and I honestly communicated what we could easily tell him and our daughters about my diagnosis. If I didn't make it, I honestly wanted my wife to find someone else to help her raise my son.

Trust your gut when it comes to the reliability, integrity, and moral fabric of the people you surround yourself with, and you will make the right choices almost every time.

Transformative lesson learned: Strive to develop relationships based on the same level of pure trust and honesty that a young child has with a parent and great things will happen.

CHAPTER 3

PERSONALIZED PROBLEM SOLVING

Earn the Privilege to Change People's Lives

Early in my career as an Investment Banker, I was given the opportunity to make a sales pitch to a pair of business partners that were interested in selling their manufacturing company. Cities Mold manufactured high precision molds that were used to make computer mice, keyboards, and larger, more complex plastic parts such as gaming consoles.

The owners of the business were two unequal partners, and they could not have been more different in terms of personalities. The majority owner, Bill, was very personable, open, honest, and quick to trust. I suspect Bill's open and honest approach with employees and customers played a meaningful role in the businesses' 25 plus years of success. While Bill lacked a college degree, he was highly skilled at understanding people, relationships, profitability, and the value of a dollar.

Everyone, from corporate client decision makers to vendors and front office staff loved Bill. He and his wife had accumulated the kind of nest egg that would allow them to retire from the daily grind and do whatever they pleased in the next chapter of their lives.

His partner, Ed, was mechanically and technically brilliant, but he could be closed off, and I found him far more difficult to read.

Unlike Bill, Ed was a man who seemed to live largely in the moment. He drove a top-of-the-line Harley to work every day that the weather allowed, dressed for his own comfort, wore his beard long, and spent his money on things and experiences geared to keeping his everyday life fun. Also, unlike his partner, he struggled with small talk or any of the other standard niceties of doing business with clients or consultants.

Ed's actions led me to believe that he was uninterested in getting to know me. But the company's shop workers and external users of their products loved Ed for all the reasons that you can imagine. He was one of them through and through.

Personal Friends, Trusted Business Partners

As I spent more time learning about the business though, I discovered three things. First, despite their differences, maybe more likely because of them, these two partners worked perfectly as a team. Bill and Ed had found a way to turn their polar opposite strengths and weaknesses into a highly productive business combination.

Second, beneath his gruff exterior, Ed was a great guy who cared deeply about the employee's well-being and the success of the business. Also, it became apparent that Ed was struggling with some very deep-seated fears related to the potential sale of the company. I initially wasn't sure what to think of Ed. Bill was easy, but I came to appreciate and enjoy both equally.

Unfortunately, it was time for Bill to move on from the business and his long standing working relationship with Ed. In many ways, it was hard for me to witness the end of something so remarkable between friends.

Prior to making my initial sales pitch, I had met with Bill and Ed a couple of times. Both mornings, I noticed that Ed walked into the meetings visibly grumpy, with his cup of coffee, and some type of on-the-fly breakfast in hand. Bill, on the other hand, walked in with a smile like he had been up for hours. Bill offered me something to drink while Ed sat down and tried to get his engine moving.

It was pretty apparent early on that Bill could read me like a book and that he was growing comfortable with me quickly. Ed seemed apprehensive, unsure, and out of his element. That really wasn't a surprise because I was dressed like an investment banker rather than a biker. As we neared the end of our second meeting, Bill said that he needed to be sure I understood something. With Ed still in the room, he explained that even though he held the majority of the company's shares, he would not make any decision unless Ed was 100% onboard.

To say I thought that was a class act thing to do between long-term friends and business partners would be an understatement. I learned something that day that I will never forget. These two business partners, despite their differences, enjoyed amazing business success largely because of their personal commitment and respect for each other regardless of the circumstances.

Trust Must Be Earned

The time came to submit my proposal and a follow-up meeting was called to walk through the details. As I suspected, by the end of my presentation I could tell Bill was onboard, but Ed was non-committal. I left the meeting somewhat confident but unsure what to expect.

Over the next three or four days I waited. I heard nothing from Bill and nothing from Ed. Late one afternoon I decided it was time to call Bill for some feedback. Sure enough, he shared that Ed was on the fence. On the fence about what, even Bill didn't know.

Over the years I have learned that some people are better than others at sorting out whether they can trust someone to sign on the dotted line and ultimately guide them to a needed solution. In thinking through the situation with Ed, I realized that I hadn't done enough to meet Ed where he was. I hadn't met his worries with the information or reassurances that he needed to be comfortable with me, professionally and personally, to say yes.

He was stuck trying to decide, and he needed something more from me.

Early the following morning I jumped in my car and headed to the company's facility with a specific plan in mind. I seemed to recall that I had seen Ed come into one of our initial meetings carrying his usual cup of coffee and a small bag from a family-owned bakery that was about four blocks from their offices. I stopped at the bakery, picked up a dozen donuts, and 2 large cups of coffee.

Prior to setting out, I had handwritten the following note to Ed:

> Ed,
>
> I understand that you are considering how to make one of the biggest personal and professional decisions of your life. I want you to know that if I am indeed entrusted to help guide you through the process, protecting your personal, professional, and financial best interests will always be priority #1 for me. My business is not about making money. It is about helping people make hard choices like the one you are now facing. Please call me

with any questions or concerns you have, and I hope you ultimately put your trust in me.

In the meantime, have a donut and a cup of coffee or two as you consider your options. I look forward to the opportunity to work with you and Bill.

Kevin

I dropped the donuts, coffee, and my handwritten note with the company's receptionist at 9:15 a.m. I hadn't even made it back to my office yet, and I had a voice message from Ed that the engagement was mine.

I was excited and relieved to hear that I was going to get the assignment. What I noticed was that I was equally excited to spend more time with Bill and Ed. They had a friendship that I wanted to be a part of, and I wanted to do what I could to ensure that friendship survived and thrived through the changes that lie ahead.

Complex Problems Simplified

All too often I see professional service providers lose sight of the fact that their main priority and challenge is to help people solve the problems that they are currently facing. Even the best business leaders have trouble making hard, complex, and often emotionally charged, decisions. I have found that to be particularly true for business owners whose personal net worth, financial security, and full-time work status could be impacted or change dramatically depending on the decision to be made.

Not only is it imperative to focus on helping business leaders make decisions, but those decisions need to be firmly grounded in the client's best interests too. When I say client, I include the internal decision maker, and the business's clients, vendors, and employees too. Those that only look at narrower short-term results without considering the big picture will make horrible mistakes. Consider the well-publicized challenges faced by EpiPen and Wells Fargo, as unjustified profit margins or sales volume incentives became far-reaching complications.

Ed was trying to sort through several emotionally charged issues. What would happen to him professionally and personally if he sold his ownership share? His best friend for the last 40 years wanted to retire. He wanted his friend to be happy. But he realized that his friend's impending retirement would impact him, his career, and his future. Facing the unknown is troubling for everyone. Ed needed to trust me to help him navigate the very uncertain, and likely unavoidable challenges that lie ahead. His temporary gridlock was understandable.

Problem, Potential Solutions, Action Items

During one stop in my career, I worked with a gentleman who was a master at putting a process and plan in place to help business leaders make complex, and many times, emotional decisions. I really could have used these insights earlier in my career to try to help Ed.

Glen followed three critical steps in engaging with new clients. Over the years, I've modified and adopted them as my own, and when I follow them, they naturally flow into the writing of a client proposal or sales presentation. But what I like most about these steps is that they can help any two people, or a team of people, figure out the best path forward.

Step 1, Problem: The most important first step is to ask questions and listen. Whether it's a partner, a client, a spouse, or a friend, sit down face-to-face and listen carefully, including how they respond to those questions. I strongly believe in face-to-face meetings and conversations because so much more can be learned. For example, when I first interviewed Bill and Ed, Ed often sat silent and fidgeted. I should have noticed that he was struggling with something and tried to sort out what that was earlier. Be aware that sometimes noticing is the same as listening. Step 1 isn't complete until both parties mutually define the core problem. That might take more than one conversation.

Step 2, Potential Solutions: Make sure to inquire about and explore the solutions that have previously been considered. You might be surprised to learn how far down the path they've gotten, but for one reason or another, they can't seem to get to the finish line. Agree on which potential solutions are viable by fleshing out the pros and cons of each. And always call out the hidden option: Do nothing. Most of the time, doing nothing is how the situation became a problem in the first place.

Step 3, Action Items: Independently pull together a thoughtful summary of your project plan for each option and your role in helping them get to the finish line. Include key action items and expected results.

Listen, Trust, Act, Solve

When working with new clients, following the three-step cadence that I outlined above funnels them to a decision to act, as the pros and cons of doing nothing are clearly laid out. It also positions the topic of fees in terms of a value proposition. Most often, once I put my clients' fears to rest that their problem will be solved and that they can trust me to guide them to a better place, the value proposition of my fees will be obvious.

The three-step problem solving process can be applied in personal relationships too. Listening and defining the core problem is always a critical first step. I think it probably goes without saying that challenges related to kids, friends, money, spouses, and careers, can be steeped in fear of the unknown or other emotions. Those potential roadblocks to moving forward need to be acknowledged but calmly set aside such that alternatives can be defined. Then take the next step to mutually agree on the specifics of proceeding to a solution.

For Ed, I moved too fast. I needed to take a step back, send him a cup of coffee, a donut, and a personal handwritten promise to help solidify his trust in me. That trust then served as the driving theme of my work for the client that led to a very successful outcome.

Transformative lesson learned: Only after personal trust has been developed will others grant you the privilege of helping them solve their most complex, sometimes emotionally challenging, problems.

CHAPTER 4

AUTHENTIC DIFFERENTIATION

The Rewards of Consistently Sharing Your True Self

The first day that I was in the hospital was filled with visitors and commotion. Christina helped me get checked in, and she stayed with me for most of the day. Then after a minor surgery to insert a catheter in my chest for the chemotherapy and other drugs to be administered, my stepmother, my kids and my Aunt Janet stopped in. They were all on their way up to my brother's cabin, which would be a much needed diversion for my kids.

I was happy to see everyone, and for an hour or so, the reality of my situation was forgotten. My kids sat on my lap, and some pictures were taken. I look at those pictures today, and I am obviously in an incredibly good mood. Being surrounded by my kids brought that out in me.

Little did I know that during all of this, my first bag of chemotherapy was already dripping into me. My chemo regimen would take six days and it included two different kinds of therapy. One was a clear liquid that took six hours, and it was easier on me. The second one, which only took about an hour to infuse, was a red liquid that I came to call red death, a nickname that said it all. I started with a dose of red death.

The side effects from that first dose weren't immediate. But as the infusion progressed, a severe headache set in, and I began to feel like someone had poured Drano directly into my stomach. The feeling was similar to, but far worse than, a Sunday morning hangover after a long night of drinking a regrettable amount of alcohol. It made sense. They were poisoning me in much the same way that an overindulgence in alcohol can poison a person.

After the dose was done, the hangover started to subside, and I recovered within two or three hours. One bag down. A victory of sorts. But I soon learned that with each progressive victory, a body becomes less resilient, the side effects last longer, and the onslaught becomes more intense.

Later that first day, my oncologist, Dr. Olson, stopped in to see me. My wife and I were in the room, and as usual, he was very upbeat with a great vibe about him. I always had a sense of calm around this guy, and I could feel that he truly was looking out for my best interests. Even so, I was fully aware that along with his success and reputation came an enormous patient caseload. I did not want to get lost in the shuffle of his patients, and as he asked me about my day, something occurred to me.

A Patient, Client, Unique Human Being

By that time in my career, I had a fair amount of experience working in the professional services industry with many clients and many different client relationships. It dawned on me that my doctor was onboarding a new client the same way as I had onboarded numerous clients of my own. And I recognized something he and I probably had in common.

In my line of work, as I am sure it was with his, there were some clients I enjoyed working with, and there were some clients I didn't. While I can honestly say that I give my best professional effort to every client, it is also true that my favorite clients get a more personal commitment that goes above and beyond professional excellence. They just do. When those clients are facing a challenge, that challenge draws on my most creative and all-encompassing energy, well past what is expected or required. I knew that I wanted to be a patient who inspired that kind of attention, care, and best work from my doctor and the hospital staff.

With Dr. Olson sitting on the edge of my bed, I looked up at him and said, "This might seem odd, but I see myself in this hospital as a client of yours. I know in my job of helping people make complicated business decisions, there are some clients I like to do work for, and some that I don't. It is important for you to realize that I want to be your best customer. If I am being a difficult patient in some way, tell me and I will change something. If you need me to eat healthier or do something else to make your job easier, let me know and I will do everything that I can to be a better patient. There are some clients of mine that I like so much that I spend my entire 45-minute drive home each night thinking about how I can do a better job for them. When you drive home each night, I hope you are thinking about how you are going to save my life. I have called a handful of people I know and trust to learn something about you, and they all say that you are fantastically gifted. I am trusting my life in your hands, and all I ask is that you try your hardest to save it."

By the end of my comments, we were both starting to get choked up. I had bared my soul to him fully and openly, and I am sure he could see I was terrified yet authentic.

He said, "When you were first diagnosed, it hit me hard. I was like wow; this guy is the same age as I am. That is all I could think about on my whole way home the other night." He smiled, put his hand on top of mine, and said "Let's see what we can do." He got up, said a few words, and he left my room.

My road to cancer survival was very long. Many times, it was unbearably lonely. I came to realize that my wife, kids, and family could not fill every void I felt or completely understand my fear. At the same time, I could not understand their fears, or fill the void I left behind. While they were by my side to help, the battle with cancer is ultimately yours alone to fight. It made me face the uncomfortable fact that each of us is born into this world alone, and when the time comes, we will leave this world alone too.

Dr. Olson was by my side for a very good chunk of my journey. While he served as my oncologist, in many ways he became my friend and cheerleader. I looked forward to every one of his visits. The professional portion of our conversations usually lasted a minute or two. The personal discussions lasted for ten minutes, and on some evenings, 45 minutes. I received the gift of getting to know him personally and professionally. I will never forget the impact that he and his personal attention had on my life.

Dare To Be Different

Like many customers, I was concerned and unsure if I had picked the right person to provide the service that I needed. I urgently needed to act and find an oncologist, so I really didn't have a choice but to move quickly and trust my instincts. Dr. Olson's reaction to my raw honesty told me I had made the right choice.

My decision to share so openly allowed me to build a powerfully positive, collaborative, relationship with my doctor. It also taught me something I had never considered before my cancer. All great working relationships – even those that are not life-and-death

— require a willingness to honestly invest one's personal self to build trust.

Conversely, when coworkers don't trust each other, silos form, collaboration falters, and "me" takes precedence over "team." Since my long journey through cancer, I have made it a point to approach every business relationship in that same way. As a result, my own capabilities, the level of personal and professional service that I provide, and my business success have all improved dramatically.

In Dr. Olson's eyes, I went from being a patient's name and number on a chart, to a human being who needed someone to help them under very tough circumstances. I made sure that he saw me as the unique person that I am. I also made sure he knew that I was invested in making his job easier, not more difficult, and his experience with me a positive, even pleasant one.

If he had been getting paid based on hours worked, I strongly suspect I wouldn't have been charged for his additional time and energy, just like I don't charge my clients for time spent thinking about their challenges on my drive home. Without fully realizing it at the time, I authentically differentiated myself from his other patients that were competing for his time as the one who was all-in trying to solve my problem in partnership with him.

Following the Herd Has Drawbacks

From time to time during my career, I have been asked to provide a competitive sales pitch to a prospective client looking to sell their business. I used to dread these. I don't anymore and I can tell you why.

A few days after going through one of these dog and pony shows, I had lunch with the attorney who asked me to present my services competing against three other providers. Mark is a friend of mine, so I asked him straight up, how I had done in my sales pitch. I was hoping for some reassurance that I was the front runner, but I was also ready for some constructive feedback. I will never forget what he said to me.

"To be honest with you Kevin, you all sounded the same. Your PowerPoint presentations all had very similar content. You are all technically sharp people, and you professionally covered the same ground regarding the likely sale price of the business. This may not be what you want to hear, but I think the decision will come down to who they like the most."

I knew Mark was trying to help me rather than criticize me, but his words made it seem like it was a crapshoot.

Sadly, I had invested hours of time and energy to technically outwork my competitors, and the result was the same one in four chances. But after some further reflection, I embraced his message that 95% of all professional service providers look and sound the same. We have all figured out the right clothes to wear, the right words to say, and how to put together a good technical sales pitch.

Yet it's the remaining 5% that sways the decision.

Ultimately, I didn't land the engagement. I knew Mark's comments were right on target. When I looked back at my presentation and approach, it was eerily similar to my competitors, and it needed to be different from my competitors. We all tried to impress the client with our technical knowledge, our financial expertise, and our intimate knowledge of the current events in the marketplace. But I overlooked the fact that most clients are looking for someone that stands out as different.

You Are the Difference

In the previous chapter, I talked about how I authentically differentiated myself by personally delivering coffee, a donut, and a handwritten promise to my prospect. I landed the engagement. During the initial interactions with my oncologist, I authentically differentiated myself from his other patients. I wasn't selling anything, yet my service as a client and personal experience working with him went from good to great. And as part of the dog and pony show sales pitch I made, I forgot to bring my true authentic self to my work and someone else got the business.

For me, being different from others isn't about winning a sales pitch, or convincing a doctor to do better work. It is about having the self-confidence to take the risk of putting your true self forward without fear of the result. Will you get burned sometimes? Yes. But oddly enough, when you do take that risk, it almost always leads to relationships becoming richer, more meaningful, and ultimately more productive.

My near-death experience taught me some hard lessons, but this lesson feels more like a gift.

Transformative lesson learned: It can be difficult, even scary, to share your true self with others, but the rewards will far outweigh the drawbacks.

CHAPTER 5

SUCCESS IS A CHOICE

Fearlessly Take the Steps Required to Increase Your Chances of Success

After my family and friends went back to their comfortable homes, I settled into the hospital. What lay ahead were several days of chemotherapy, a constant stream of nurses and other hospital staff poking and prodding me, and the inescapable reality that I was surrounded by other patients fighting for their lives or losing the battle. To call my new environment depressing was an understatement. I felt physically okay, but I could feel the negative energy that now surrounded me.

For the first day or two, much of my own energy went toward trying to digest what had happened. A week prior I was sleeping in a comfortable bed in a beautiful house on 2.5 acres of land. I shared meals with my family every day, and watched a variety of birds, deer, and other wildlife from our kitchen table. Life was very good.

Now I sat in a hospital room with pale gray walls, no windows, cold tile floors, and food that was hard to eat even on days when I didn't have a chemo hangover. Who wouldn't feel a bit down in the dumps? I started feeling like I was in jail, and I knew I had to break out of the funk. I needed a lift, and to restore some sense of normalcy to rekindle at least a glimmer of hope.

One day, as I was eating breakfast, my nurse came in and hung another bag of chemotherapy to drip into me. I dreaded the thought of the next six hours ahead. I couldn't just sit there, waiting for the reality of my current circumstances to pull me into sadness and depression. I couldn't stand the idea of my fellow cancer inmates, each trapped in our respective jail cells, all of us on edge and fighting for our lives.

I remembered a sign I first saw when I checked into the hospital directing visitors to the maternity floor. Just seeing that sign had brought me back to the remarkable experience of the birth of my three kids in a similar hospital. I will never forget each of their birthdays. I decided that if I was going to make it through a six-hour chemotherapy infusion with my sanity intact, I needed to spend at least a few hours in a much happier place in the hospital than the sterile room that I felt stuck in.

Clouds of Depression to Clear Blue Sky

When my nurse returned to check on me, I asked, "Would it be okay to leave my room for a while?"

She asked the obvious question, "Where do you intend to go?"

I responded, "I need to get out of my room. It's depressing sitting here all day."

"That's fine. But please be back in your room when your dose of chemotherapy is done so I can check your vital signs. You really should enjoy some freedom from your room now. The chemotherapy will significantly compromise your immune system over the next few days, and once that happens, you won't be able to leave your room anymore."

That was all I needed to hear. I was already in sweatpants and a sweatshirt as I refused to wear a hospital gown, so I was ready to run.

I grabbed my IV pole with the chemo bag, and I broke out of jail for a few hours. As I walked off the floor, I could tell the nurses and other staff were not used to seeing patients leave their rooms in the Oncology Department. Once most patients check in, they stay in their room until they are escorted out in a wheelchair or something worse. I didn't want to be surrounded by death much less consumed by it.

I walked right to the elevator, took it down to the first floor, and I quickly found the directions to the maternity floor. I got right back in the elevator and went back up to a different floor and a vastly different world.

As soon as I got off the elevator, I found the viewing window where the newborns were being fed and cared for while their new mothers got some much-needed rest. My whole perspective and attitude changed in an instant.

The Power of Optimistic Energy

I found a small sitting area and soaked it in. The walls were painted bright colors to welcome the expectant families and newborns. There were balloons, flowers, and stuffed teddy bears near the nurse's station, waiting to be delivered or given to the nurses as there were already too many gifts for a small room. Happy fathers and extended families were celebrating, smiling, and laughing in the hallways. On my floor, flowers could not even enter patient rooms as they could bring in mold or other dangerous contaminants capable of killing the patients. An oncology room is a sterile environment by every definition.

I spent every moment I could outside of my hospital room and away from the Oncology Department. One day, I shot baskets with a hospital employee in a physical therapy gymnasium two hours after finishing a round of chemotherapy. I thought I might pass out or throw up while shooting, but it was worth it. Over the course of treatments, I walked many miles in and around the hospital. The fall colors and sunshine outside were a welcome relief from the depressing gray walls of my hospital room. One evening, I missed my nightly call to my kids because I was engrossed in a long conversation with my brother in the cafeteria. My wife, frantic and afraid that I had passed out somewhere, convinced the nurses to track me down, even having me paged over the hospital wide loudspeaker.

Intuitively, I could feel the Oncology Department pulling me in the wrong direction, so I consistently pushed myself toward a brighter light. Since that experience, I have been a part of, or witnessed, several personal and professional situations where you could just feel that something needed to change to ensure a positive outcome.

Business Cancer Diagnosis and Treatment

After several years focused on closing financial, business, and real estate transactions, I had an opportunity to join a financially underperforming manufacturing company. It appeared to be a perfect fit as it would allow me to help set the strategic direction of the company in collaboration with the president, while leading the effort to change the trajectory of the company's profitability.

Unfortunately, the change in financial performance had to start with a change in some of the company's senior leadership and the business's overall culture as the rank and file were clearly frustrated working in the negative energy at the company.

Within the first two months of my employment, the owner of the business re-engaged in the business from afar. He quickly determined that the mood of the company was pessimistic and asked the president to step down. Seeing anyone lose their job is hard to watch. But I am also painfully aware of the alternative when the wrong talent is in a leadership position: the organization and teamwork suffer, hard-working people become unmotivated, and highly skilled people either find other jobs or lose their jobs as the business unwinds.

The president's departure led to two other employees choosing to resign shortly thereafter. As CFO, I gained a clear view of why those changes needed to happen. While the three senior people who left were great people, they had lost their way as the company lost its direction. They had stopped doing the right things to make the company successful.

Some sure signs of that included travel to see prospective customers that revolved around when non-business-related tee times were available. Dinners and drinks with long-standing industry friends that had become completely divorced from generating revenue were also too common. As other internal employees figured out what was happening, company morale sank even further.

At a breathtaking pace, the owner of this business recognized that something needed to change and acted. I knew the owner was right, but I was too inexperienced at the time to move as fast as he did. He had successfully operated several businesses, and I am sure he knew that if he removed one bad apple that other bad apples would fall off the tree too.

Once the underperforming employees were removed, the business quickly pivoted and began hiring the type of people and talent needed to become successful. After a year or two of team building, the mood and energy level at the company changed dramatically. And business losses turned the corner to financial success.

Once the dust settled a bit, I recalled some very simple, yet insightful advice I received in college from my 100-level marketing professor. One day, after entering the classroom and sitting on top of a student's desk, he said, "If I were to give you all some words of wisdom, during your business careers I encourage you to make sure you surround yourself with people who are successful rather than with people who are on their way to failure."

The owner of this business had intuitively followed my marketing professor's advice. Now when I encounter negative energy rooted in questionable behavior, I take action at the same breathtaking speed too.

Rising to the Challenge

Someone once asked me how I beat cancer knowing that I had come through many days and months of feeling totally depleted and out of energy. I have thought about that question a lot. I can point to three specific things that helped me get to the finish line.

First, I made a conscious choice to survive, and then I turned beating cancer into a challenge or a goal to strive for. If I let myself see cancer as an insurmountable death sentence, it no doubt would have become one. There is strength in taking control of one's own destiny, so I took control of all aspects of my disease as an important step toward meeting my goal.

Second, I have come to realize that a goal will go unmet unless I surround myself with what it takes to meet it. I had a great doctor, and the nursing staff were second to none. My core care team clearly cared about my survival, and they had formed a personal bond based on consistent communication and trust between them. I was lucky to be part of their team. We all just happened to be confined to a work environment that was not supportive of a successful outcome for me. So, I removed that obstacle as often as I could.

Third, I relentlessly refused to accept defeat. Is it reasonable to expect that every cancer patient will survive? No. But I was going to go down swinging if I didn't.

Transformative lesson learned: If you believe that you can create a path to beat anything that life throws at you, you can expect many successes. Alternatively, if you accept defeat when faced with adversity, failure is a certainty.

CHAPTER 6

IT TAKES A TEAM

*When Friends, Acquaintances, and Co-workers
Pierced My Independent Silo*

When I first checked into the hospital, I really didn't like the idea of being assigned to a small room. I was even more uncomfortable with the idea that I might have to share a small room with another patient. I would have paid a lot of money to have my own room and space. Somehow, the idea of losing even a few square feet of what I could call my own felt especially defeating.

As it turned out, I was indeed assigned a very small room, but there would be no roommate. It hadn't even occurred to me that my treatment would include killing off my body's ability to fight even the smallest infection so completely that being around another patient 24/7 had never been an option. In the upside-down world of cancer treatment, I took that news as a stroke of good luck.

A few days after my chemotherapy regimen began, one of my closest co-workers, Maryann, came to visit me. Most days at our brokerage firm, Maryann and I were joined at the hip as we both represented business owners who hired us to sell their ownership interests. Because we were so close, Maryann knew me well, including my addiction to just about all desserts, especially chocolate chip cookies. For her first trip to come see me, she arrived armed with two dozen assorted cookies from my favorite small bakery in downtown Minneapolis.

It was great to see Maryann, and strangely interesting to hear what was happening in the office. Crazy as it sounds, my hospitalization was a welcome break from the daily grind of my career. But neither of us had predicted the impact that the initial doses of chemotherapy would have on my ability to taste or tolerate one of my favorite foods. She presented the cookies, and I anxiously took my first bite.

I was taken aback by the taste. Instead of bringing a familiar jolt of enjoyment to my taste buds, that first bite brought me right to the edge of throwing up, which was followed by more waves of nausea. I felt horrible for Maryann, as I could not hide my reaction.

Despite my disappointment, I thanked Maryann profusely for the thought she put into her gift. It meant a lot to me that she knew me so well and took the time to bring me something that had always brought me happiness. Instead of being the treat she intended, though, those cookies ended up being a reminder that I was tragically losing something I loved. In this case, it was the taste of food, and the simple pleasure of sugar.

It was both disappointing and depressing. I didn't know it at the time, but the ability to taste cookies was only one of many things I would ultimately need to let go after my diagnosis. The minute that she left, I set the cookies aside, but I could not face the thought of throwing away something I loved so much.

Maryann was one of a handful of people who consistently visited me at the hospital. Her visits made me appreciate that people wanted to help me in any way that they could, yet for some reason, I was initially uncomfortable accepting their help. Upon reflection, I realized that I needed to come out of my own silo and let others join my team in the fight rather than going it alone.

An Unexpected Team Member

Later that day, my room was due for its daily cleaning. I noticed the same employee, Lorraine, cleaned my room everyday Monday through Friday. Her name stuck with me as it was the same as my sister in-law. Lorraine looked to be in her early sixties, and despite what appeared to be an extremely tedious job, she was always in a good mood. She had been working at the hospital for over 25 years.

Lorraine's day-to-day work consisted of mopping, cleaning, and dusting every nook and cranny of the floor, counter tops, and bathroom in my room. Once she was done in my room, she moved on to the next one. Lorraine openly loved her job, and given how important it was to keep the patient rooms sterile, I was grateful to see her every day. What I didn't recognize at the time was how much Lorraine cared about the patients, including me, and how much sway she had at the hospital.

One afternoon, after she finished up her daily routine, Lorraine unexpectedly asked me a question, "I have seen that you have a wife, friends and three little kids that come to see you. There is a much bigger room at the end of the hall that I was told I need to do a more thorough cleaning of tomorrow because that patient is being discharged. If you want to move to the best room on the floor, I think I can work with the nursing staff to make that happen. Would that be ok with you?"

Without hesitation I said, "That would be fantastic." What was fantastic was that Lorraine had paid that much attention to me, my wife, friends, and kids.

The next afternoon, I was moved to a room that was at least twice the size of the one I was originally assigned to. It was still a one-person room, but the extra space made a huge difference over the next two plus weeks in solitary confinement. Just before lunch, Sharon, my nurse for the day, confirmed the move would be happening.

While lying in my hospital bed, I was wheeled to my new room right after lunch. When I arrived and saw Lorraine just finishing up cleaning with a huge grin on her face, I recognized that what brought great meaning to her job wasn't the cleaning.

The next day, during her cleaning routine, Lorraine had to move my box of cookies that had migrated with me to the new room. I wanted her to know that I saw something more in her than her daily work too. When she picked up the box, I asked her if she would like to have one. She looked surprised at first. Then I quickly convinced her that they were from a great bakery in downtown Minneapolis and that she needed to try one. She reluctantly opened the box and took one.

Every day, Lorraine came into my room. Every day, I looked forward to seeing her. She didn't hold an executive level job at the hospital, but our connection and her commitment to me and my experience in the hospital will never be forgotten.

Leadership Without the Title

I have been lucky enough to meet and work with many talented people. What has really separated good teams from great teams have been those people willing to develop strong, mutually beneficial, collaborative working relationships within the organization and outside of the organization too. Granted, not every employee is going to possess the exact level of skill, experience, and ability you envision for their role. But 99% of employees are "good eggs," and all "good eggs" bring a valuable perspective to a highly functioning team.

I once worked with a man who was one of the most purely giving and unselfish people I have met. In fact, Ben may have been giving to a fault, which was a subject we often talked about, as some of his co-workers took advantage of his selflessness. Ben's main charge was to ensure the quality of the products being produced for our industrial manufacturing company. Striving for quality perfection in a manufacturing process isn't easy. At times, his job could be thankless. Ben fielded and helped to solve customer complaints along with a long list of other responsibilities that he naturally took the lead on.

Over time I came to appreciate just how far-reaching Ben's influence on the company was. He had developed such strong working connections within every department that whenever I needed better insights into a situation or problem, all I had to do was talk to Ben. He had his fingers on the pulse of everything.

Ben was professional in everything that he did. He had a unique sense for when to push people, and when to sit back and let things run their course. Cynics might dismiss that skill as politically savvy, but I don't think Ben had a political bone in his body. He simply did his best to do the right thing for all stakeholders consistently. Although it's been years since we worked together, he has remained someone that I am envious of. But I must admit, I am still a work-in-process in terms of adopting all of his gifts regarding patience and working with people.

The real proof of Ben's value to the company slowly became apparent when he left his position to attend to a personal family crisis. Sales volume didn't drop immediately. The team continued to ship quality products out the door. And for a few months, all seemed to be fine. But then a variety of problems started to crop up.

The glue that held the business together started to come apart.

Communication between department leaders had begun to suffer as a skilled facilitator and moderator was no longer in place. The resulting periodic breakdowns in communications led to unproductive infighting and finger pointing. This inevitably impacted teamwork and inter-departmental trust. If Ben committed to the sales rep, the customer, and corporate leadership that a client quality issue would be addressed and solved by Friday at noon, the problem was solved by noon on Friday.

Ben had a knack for bringing all parties together and motivating them to work as a team to hit a desired goal or deadline. Ben did not have any formal authority over any of the people involved in meeting often tricky deadlines. Yet he always rallied those around him to the shared goals. I was consistently in awe by what he could get done.

The Power of Teamwork

Unfortunately, people who make it to the executive level of a company all too often lose sight of the other employees that are down below them on the org chart. Maybe it is pure ego, or maybe it is an overriding insecurity that someone will second guess them or do a better job than they can.

What is important to recognize is that a team isn't formed when a coach forces people together and tells them what to do. A team forms when all its members believe they're all on the same mission, and that they both trust each other, and are inspired by each other, to do the right thing to get there.

I came to see Maryann and Lorraine as part of my care team. They were both focused on doing what they could to help me beat cancer, and I was obviously engaged in that goal too. I never considered myself to be a selfish person, but their unselfish acts of kindness were impressive. Ben had many of the same traits. He rallied friends and co-workers toward a common goal, and we all trusted him implicitly in the process.

When a group comes together and puts a higher priority on us rather than me, great things happen.

Transformative lesson learned: An army of like-minded people that bands together as a team to achieve a common goal will far outperform an individual who is uncomfortable or unwilling to accept help from others.

CHAPTER 7

THE CANCER OF INFIGHTING

Pushing Through Corporate Infighting to Receive the Hospital Care I Deserved

Checking into a hospital for an undefined length of time is a nerve-racking experience. But I was committed to making the most of it. To state the obvious: I was not feeling 100 percent, especially after getting each dose of chemotherapy. But my life wasn't over yet. In fact, in some ways, being taken care of 24/7 and leaving the stress and anxiety of nearly every other aspect of life at the hospital's front door wasn't all bad. On days when I did feel good in the hospital, I had a lot of energy and drive to do or learn something.

Within the first few days of my initial hospital stay, I learned that I would be assigned what was called a Prime Nurse. Each patient is given a Prime Nurse to help ensure that patients receive consistent care, and that family members have a single point of contact. Obviously, Prime Nurses don't work 24/7, so I had many different nurses assigned to me. It didn't take long to figure out that a truly great Prime Nurse built personal connections with their patients, tending to their emotional ups and downs, as well as their physical condition.

I couldn't have hoped for a better Prime Nurse than Sharon. She was extremely engaged, emotionally aware, and attentive. Yet she gave me my space too. Over time, I learned that she had been a college volleyball coach prior to going into nursing, and that she loved every aspect of the sport, from teaching and playing, to mentoring young athletes. But as she grew a bit older, married, and started a family, the travel and minimal pay started to become too much of a burden. So, she went back to school and earned her nursing degree. By the time I met her, she had spent a decade as a nurse in the Oncology Department.

One day I asked her why she chose oncology. She said it was amazing to witness life events and "miracles" that happened there. Sharon told me about a patient who was given hours to live yet remained alive and alert for over two weeks. Despite that patient's total awareness that death was near, she was bright, happy, and engaged with the hospital staff, family, and friends until her last breath.

We also talked openly about how difficult many patients and family members could be. Fear of the unknown and stress will do that sometimes. While that was not always easy for Sharon, she said being with people who were faced with the possibility of death inspired her every day.

In getting to know Sharon a bit personally, and in the same vein as my oncologist, I wanted to make sure I made her life as easy as possible too. I figured if I was happy and engaging rather than bitter and cranky, she would be willing to spend more time with me, which made my day go faster. To be clear, there were days that I was distressed, unhappy, and kept to myself, but being a crabby pain in the butt wasn't good for anyone. And, talking to people who enjoyed my company was going to make me a whole lot happier than sitting there alone, so my approach to make the best of things was win/win.

For the first week or ten days, all went perfectly with Sharon serving as my Prime Nurse. I saw her five days a week, and we got to know each other quite a bit. Our daily conversations and interactions didn't just help to pass the time. They gave me insights into the medical profession, patient care, health crises, death and dying, and so much more. These topics were pretty much foreign to me prior to my diagnosis. Sharon spent time with my wife Christina when she could be with me at the hospital too. But then, inexplicably, I stopped seeing Sharon.

The Problem That Shouldn't Have Been A Problem

At first, I assumed Sharon had a few days of PTO. A few days turned into a few more days until she unexpectedly stopped in my room. Sharon didn't write her name on the white board which is the first task for each new nursing shift. Instead, she approached my bed and asked how I was doing. After we exchanged a few words, she broke the news to me that she would no longer be my Prime Nurse. Oddly enough, that role was going to be rotated between members of the nursing staff going forward. I asked why? She hesitated, then peeked out in the hallway before coming back to talk more freely.

Sharon explained that some of the other nurses had picked up on how easy I was to take care of, and that they had complained to the Charge Nurse (the head of all oncology nurses) that Sharon was getting the easiest patient. Basically, Sharon had been pulled as my Prime Nurse so others could spend their shift with the easy patient.

Consider the ugly irony in that outcome. As a result of my efforts to be the best partner I could be for the hospital team helping me, I was rewarded with a lower quality of nursing care. And indeed, my quality of nursing care decreased from that day forward. The word "disappointment" does not come close to how I felt about that change. I felt like something was wrongly taken away from me, and it was hard not to get angry. The rotation of other nurses did a great job of taking care of my physical health, but in some ways, I was left to take care of my emotional health on my own.

Over the next few months, I found a workaround to the hospital's internal disputes by making a point to get to know the other members of the staff. One nurse in particular, Kim, was great. We both loved to give each other a hard time about just about anything and everything. Kim worked part-time nights because she had two young daughters that she wanted to spend time with during the days.

Often, when Kim came into my room to check my vital signs, I was half-asleep because it was 2:00 a.m. But I was quickly wide awake and ready to "thank her" profusely for making my sleep patterns miserable. Late one evening, when the nurses were having a potluck dinner in the staff lounge, Kim snuck me into the lounge and encouraged me to take a plate with anything that might taste good. Nothing tasted good, given the side effects of chemotherapy. But that wasn't the point and I suspect Kim knew it. She was helping me break the rules. Given my lack of immune system at the time, who knows what level of health risk I took eating from a potluck spread, but I am not always the greatest rule follower. Kim wasn't either.

Fair and Equitable Problem Solving

I learned firsthand how corporate politics and infighting can infiltrate every workplace. Even when human lives are at stake.

Let's face it, infighting starts early in life. Young siblings fight and disagree at home just like adult co-workers can bicker, complain, and undermine each other in the office. Parents and corporate leadership need to be upfront, consistent, and confident in how problems are addressed, or "the inmates start to run the asylum."

All too often, my career has given me a ringside seat to this dynamic. In working with a significant number of family-owned or closely held businesses, there are days when I think I have seen it all in terms of helping solve disagreements between family members and partners. And then I am surprised by a new challenge, situation, and solution.

For a period of years, I served on the advisory board to a business whose founding father and mother were committed to passing on ownership and leadership of the organization to the second generation and beyond. To be completely honest, I was pessimistic at first that they could be successful in their efforts. But the longer I worked on the project, the more I came to realize that my pessimism stemmed from my own family history, not theirs.

I too grew up in a family-owned business. My dad started his manufacturing company early in his career, and my first job consisted of sweeping factory floors, part-time, when I was ten years old. I had three older siblings, and while three of us four saw the world in a very similar way, I came to appreciate over time that my sister and I were very different. Still today, I wish our relationship could be better than it is, but I have also accepted that the gap between us is too wide to be consistently bridged. My dad could have attempted to transition his business to the four of us, but I think the chances of success would have been next to zero given the inevitable disagreements and infighting that would have occurred.

My client's family dynamics were very different from mine. The parents were tied at the hip in making every decision. They were also unwavering as a unified front once decisions were made, and they were both extremely committed to each member of the family equally. Generation two had many of the same traits.

During advisory board meetings, the two generations openly talked through current family and business issues until resolutions were defined. What's more, they encouraged the outside advisors to present hypothetical challenges that the family could or would face in the future. I was not part of what happened behind closed doors outside of our meetings, but when they emerged, I was in awe of how the family successfully worked through their differences. I never saw even a small crack in the family's commitment to reaching their goal of transferring the leadership and ownership of their family-owned business.

It has been more than a decade since my assignment with the family ended, but I recently ran into two of the brothers. Their business continues to thrive under generation two's leadership.

Diagnose, Treat, Cure

I have worked with many business leaders and leadership teams who have suffered from dysfunctional or disruptive behavior in their offices. Those behaviors need to be nipped in the bud, but all too frequently they fester instead. I see leaders who are pretty good at recognizing the issue. Those same leaders are at times quite good at taking steps that appear to be headed toward resolving the issue. But for some reason, they shy away from confronting the people causing the problem, and when appropriate, levying consequences for their actions.

When I heard that my Prime Nurse was being removed as the point person of my nursing care, I knew that the leadership of the nursing staff punted rather than addressing the real issue. The result was that the level of patient care declined, which I strongly suspect conflicts with what the senior hospital staff prides itself in. In contrast, my client successfully transitioned the ownership and leadership of their business to the second generation by confronting their challenges head-on. The mother and father had a consistently strong hand in making sure the family met its goals, and their business remains strong today.

You will never solve, and productive teamwork will rarely survive, counterproductive behavior if you pretend it's normal and hope that it will go away on its own. It won't. Boundaries and expectations need to be set and enforced consistently. And if someone leaves the team because they are fairly called on the carpet for playing games, so be it. The rest of the organization will win when they see they have leadership they can trust to do the right thing for the good of the team in all circumstances.

Transformative lesson learned: Internal corporate politics are no different than cancer. They need to be diagnosed and treated with urgency or their malignancy will aggressively spread.

CHAPTER 8

PROACTIVELY INVEST IN RELATIONSHIPS

The More I Explored the Topic of Relationships, the More I Learned About Life

My near-death experience with cancer validated my long-standing belief in the importance of relationships at home, in the office, and as part of one's life legacy. It also brought me to further appreciate what it takes to be truly open, honest, and vulnerable with the people that I choose to surround myself with. I used to be afraid to put myself out there and tell someone how I felt. Now I more easily open-up without fear, as I know life is not worth living without taking the inherent risk of disappointment or lack of reciprocation that every relationship comes with.

I don't think anyone is born with innately perfect relationship skills. I know I wasn't. In fact, my relationship and communication skills have always been a work in progress. I hate to admit it, but I make mistakes all too often. When that happens, I try to own the problem I created, work hard to make things right, and hopefully get back to building on something versus watching the relationship become permanently frayed or fade away. I attempt to hold myself to these ideals whether I am interacting with my wife, kids, close friends, or a business partner.

Relationships of any kind have bumps in the road, and while I wish I could avoid all of them, sometimes I fall right into a pothole instead.

Several years ago, I was entirely focused on helping entrepreneurs transition the ownership of their businesses. I had established a reputation as the guy to bring in when a company needed to be strategically positioned and branded as part of maximizing its value in the marketplace. After thirteen years in that space, I was ready for a change. In many ways, I felt like I had accomplished what I wanted to do, and I needed a new challenge. I couldn't see spending the remaining 15 or 20 years of my career on the same worn path.

I began a search to find an opportunity to leverage my financial and strategic expertise. I wanted to roll up my sleeves as a full-time employee and improve my somewhat raw skills as a business operator with a particular interest in helping a company significantly improve its profitability and market value. I landed at the company I first told you about in Chapter 4, a 35-person manufacturing company that had experienced relatively flat financial performance for a handful of years running.

I knew the company had an ambiguous plan for growth as I had been hired by the company's president to perform a small consulting project a few years earlier. I also had a sense that there were some leadership and internal employee challenges through conversations I had with the president during the hiring process that never quite seemed to add up. I was optimistic that stepping in as its VP of Corporate Development & CFO to drive business growth and change the course of the business's profitability would be an interesting challenge for me. At least that is what I believed when I walked in the door on my first day.

I pretty much expected to confirm that the company was not on a consistent growth curve. It was nice to see that it wasn't on the path to near-term failure either. What I didn't quite fully appreciate is the strong hand of the absentee, majority owner. He was passionate about revenue and profit growth, and from the get-go, he relentlessly voiced his frustration with the business's current level of stagnation. That frustration reached an inflection point when less than three months into my tenure, he fired the company's president, adding many responsibilities to my already full workload.

What followed were several months of constant, sometimes chaotic, change. Periodic conversations with the absentee owner became lengthy, daily calls. His main message was simple. He expected me to push others hard to shake up the entrenched culture of the company and to get the business back on a profitable growth trajectory as soon as possible.

In many ways, I agreed with his directive. Something needed to change. But I did not agree with his abrasive messaging or approach. In fact, despite his brilliance, I thought he often belittled or downplayed the skills and insights of others.

Many times, I found myself trying to juggle the owner's constant pushing, my desire to step into a leadership gap, while also considering the two remaining leadership team members that I needed to work with day-to-day, Roger and Pete.

After working for twelve years as a standalone, revenue-producing M&A professional, I came to realize that I had some real weaknesses in interpersonal skills and team building. I often became the messenger of bad news. And in that role, rather than soften or modify the owner's message, it was not uncommon for me to pass it on to Roger and Pete as my own. In doing that, I offended two important people, a mistake I came to regret.

One Step Forward, Two Steps Back

I could tell that Roger and Pete were extremely talented individuals. Both held critical positions at the company, and while I could plainly see that the business needed them, I also had an owner who adamantly believed that they were part of the problem. Roger and Pete were part of the problem in some ways. But I found myself walking a tightrope between the man who signed my paycheck and two guys that I didn't know particularly well. In retrospect, I should have invested more time upfront to get to know Roger and Pete better as rebuilding their trust took a long time once I made some missteps.

Over the course of two or three years I had some open and hard discussions with Roger and Pete as I could tell something was wrong. I learned that I had started off on the wrong foot by being brought on by the previous president. Neither of them was asked to interview me as part of the hiring process, and neither of them had a lot of trust or respect for the former leader. Unfortunately, their perspective regarding the owner's ability to make the best choices was tainted too. In a nutshell, they felt disrespected.

I compounded Roger and Pete's mistrust by pushing them in ways that felt degrading to them. In my eagerness to make business changes quickly, I anxiously moved forward with what I saw as critical action items without fully gaining their input or buy-in. They each had invested more than ten years of blood, sweat, and tears into the company and I had been there for a few months. How could I possibly know more than they did?

As Roger and Pete's frustrations with me became clearer, I was compelled to repair the problems that I had created. I did my best to hear them out and learn from their history with the company, while soaking up as much of their tribal knowledge as I could. I learned a lot. I agreed with much of what they said, and the decisions going forward were better because of their input. Did we always see eye to eye with each other after that? No. We continued to have some differences. That was to be expected and just fine.

Business Relationships and Development

It was at this point in my career that I started to think more critically about relationships, and the requirements for a successful partnership both at home and in the office. What I've come to believe is that all mutually productive relationships pass through the same four stages. I like to think of these stages in terms typically assigned to courtship and marriage.

Stage 1: Introduction
Stage 2: Dating
Stage 3: Differences & Compromise
Stage 4: Trusted Partner

Introduction: The stage name speaks for itself. Two people or a team of people are introduced to each other. The introduction may be in person, at a restaurant, or over a virtual meeting. The early stages of any relationship are new, exciting, and full of hope and promise.

Dating: This is the stage where people begin to sort things out. The new and exciting part might cloud people's judgment as hope and promise continue to prevail. But, without developing some level of trust, many relationships end here.

Differences & Compromise: The dreaded first argument or disagreement happens. It might be a quality problem raised by a customer who just received a delivery of critical parts. Or worse, an employee or customer frustration that is unvoiced, but simmers, unresolved. Hopefully there is an initial foundation of trust in place already such that differences can be honestly and respectfully voiced. By working together to compromise and solve problems, it's possible to come back together stronger than ever.

Trusted Partner: For those relationships that survive stages 1-3, this is where everything starts to gel. The team is rowing in sync. Products and services meet all expectations. The boat is headed in the right direction, and all involved trust each other to work toward mutually productive goals and outcomes.

Relationship Selling & Sales Management

More recently in my career, I came across the phrase "customer intimacy." After exploring that concept, I continued to build on how the stages of relationship development apply to different facets of business. Today, when I assess the progress of a newly hired salesperson, I consider the following:

Introduction	Is the new salesperson effectively getting out in the marketplace and making new business connections?
Dating	How many of those connections are progressing toward a collaborative working relationship and ultimately a growth in company revenue?

Differences and Compromise	When customer problems arise, how effective are they at giving where needed, pushing back where needed, and ultimately solving the problem? Are their relationships stronger after the fact, strained, or broken?
Trusted Partner	Is the salesperson consistently being referred to other customers?

Over the course of my career, I have read many how-to books about the importance of relationships within the sales function of an organization. It's a lot tougher to find much written regarding the importance of relationships in the non-sales areas of a company.

Vendor & Employee Management

Consider the investment of time and energy it takes when you need to replace a critical vendor, such as an outsourced IT provider. The introduction stage can be exciting. After hearing a carefully targeted sales pitch, it is very easy to get optimistic that you will soon receive the technical support and service that you need. But shortly after onboarding the new vendor, reality creeps back into the picture.

New IT providers are often faced with a steep learning curve as they sort out the specifics of back-up procedures, unique business software, and the idiosyncrasies of each employee's needs when they call into the help desk. Patience is required from all parties, as it's unrealistic to think that the new vendor already knows everything about its new client. If all goes according to plan, and after a few hiccups are smoothed over, the new IT provider settles in as your trusted business partner a year or two later.

These same stages occur with a new banking relationship, accountant, or attorney. With very few exceptions, it can take months, if not years, for a new vendor to reach the pinnacle of performance. So, choose carefully. And invest your time and effort into building a long-term highly performing relationship knowing that a break-up can be painful.

Last, but likely most important, is the relationship that a manager has with an employee. Again, consider the stages that all new employees must pass through prior to becoming high performing team members. It's great to interview and finally find someone to hire. But once that person is onboard, and the honeymoon is over, it's rare that the new employee has entered the job as a perfect fit. New employees need to be trained, mentored, and at times, some awkward discussions are needed to guide the employee in the right direction.

But, as I learned in my experience with Roger and Pete, it's very important to recognize that it's a two-way street. For every "imperfection" a manager sees in their new hire, the new hire is also seeing flaws in their new manager. Like every relationship, both parties must see the value and benefit of working at it. That includes being receptive to hearing constructive criticism when appropriate. And if there isn't a foundation of trust between the manager and the employee, ongoing discussions can become tense and unproductive.

Recognition, Effort and Commitment

The seismic changes in how business is conducted over the past twenty years have made the awareness of these four stages of customer, vendor, and employee relationship development more relevant than ever. If you doubt me, consider today's digital marketplace.

We now work in an environment where person-to-person contact is virtually obsolete for increasing the volume of small ticket retail and corporate sales. It has also forced entire organizations to recognize and nurture trust through digitized communication with not only their customers, but with their employees too. What's more, we all too often employ social monitoring, surveying, and other ways to "listen" to customers, employees, and vendors. While I believe many of these changes are here to stay, I also believe we need to be thoughtful in how we manage them.

One last thing to consider is the amount of time it takes for a business relationship to mature into a trusted partnership. A relationship with a new team member or vendor may take months rather than years because the interactions are typically more frequent. It can take three to five years for a relationship-driven salesperson to truly hit their stride, as it is harder to get in front of new customers with any consistency.

Oddly enough, most romantic relationships take about the same amount of time to move from dating to trusted partner. In all cases, it takes time, effort, and personal commitment to get there. And once we find a trusted partner at work or at home, keep in mind that the work is not over.

I ran into some potholes with Roger and Pete early on. My desire to impress the owner compounded those issues, turning those small potholes into a full-blown road construction project. It required a lot of time and energy to fix those missteps and make things right. From there, we had our differences, but we always found ways to work through them. I am grateful to Roger and Pete for setting aside their frustrations. They were willing to invest in our working relationship, rather than giving up on me. It was all well worth it.

Transformative lesson learned: My career, my personal life, and my legacy will be defined by my ability to develop and maintain relationships with trusted partners.

CHAPTER 9

MORAL COMPASS OVER MONEY

Even the Best Doctors Can Lose Sight of the Goal of Saving Lives

The gift I received when I was first diagnosed with cancer arrived in July of 2001. For more reasons than I can count, I saw it as a gift then, and I still see it as a gift today. From the beginning, I considered having cancer a challenge rather than a death sentence, which was a huge plus. I like challenges! In fact, I believe holding onto an attitude that "I can beat this" versus "my destiny is out of my control" helped me in many ways.

During my downtime in the hospital getting chemotherapy and recovering from the effects, I started planning a solo canoe trip into the Boundary Waters Canoe Area. For those of you that aren't familiar, the BWCA is a one-million-acre wilderness area in the most northern part of Minnesota. There are hundreds of lakes, rivers, and ponds to explore. It is remote, often rugged, and a perfect place to quietly reconnect with nature. You might come face-to-face with a bear, but it's unlikely you will see a cell phone tower.

I had previously taken one other short trip to the BWCA that consisted of canoeing one mile across a lake, portaging the canoe and gear about a quarter of a mile, and pitching a tent on a second lake. This time around I wanted to travel at least 20 miles into the wilderness.

It is highly suggested that you learn how to use a compass before you get to the BWCA, as getting lost in the middle of nowhere is a real risk. As I sat in my hospital bed planning my adventure. I didn't own a compass, much less know how to use one. I guess I figured if I happen to survive cancer, I could survive anything. My wife and family probably thought I was crazy, and I suppose prayed that I would never actually do it. But I needed a goal and something to look forward to.

After recovering from five rounds of chemotherapy that started with my diagnosis in August of 2001, I returned to work part-time in March of 2002. I transitioned to full-time two months later, and I started to feel a little bit normal. In mid-September of 2002, slightly more than one year after my odyssey began, I drove to northern Minnesota and pushed my solo canoe off the shoreline. It was a staggering feeling of accomplishment and recovery. It was emotionally overwhelming, too.

I never did take the time to learn how to use a compass, and within an hour, I became slightly lost portaging between lakes and streams. Luckily, I found my way after a few anxious moments. By day three, I needed two lengthy naps, as canoeing several miles to a new spot, fishing for food, setting up camp, cutting wood, and cooking my meals was exhausting. I woke up the morning of day four at 4:00 a.m., wearing everything that I brought with me, shivering with frost on my sleeping bag. I canoed back to civilization under a clear blue sky without a breath of wind blowing or the smallest ripple on the lake. I have taken some amazing vacations in my life, and none of them can hold a candle to that one.

The Marathon Continues

Unfortunately, eight months after my trip to the BWCA, my cancer returned in May of 2003. I learned of my fate on the Friday before Memorial weekend, and I checked back into the hospital the Tuesday after Memorial Day. The biggest challenge of my life started all over again. But I had a good relationship with my oncologist, Dr. Olson, and I still remembered many of the nursing staff in the hospital. At least I could look forward to reconnecting with all of them.

The first step was to get my disease under control again. That meant three weeks in the hospital and a debilitating round of chemotherapy. To say it was a physical and emotional challenge would be a vast understatement. It was excruciatingly cruel. About a week into it, I started developing a fever. At 10:00 a.m., my temperature was 99.5 degrees, and I could feel a freight train coming. By 11:30 a.m., my temperature was 104.1 degrees and the freight train hit me head-on. Without an immune system, my body had no fight.

Luckily, my fever capped out, but that afternoon and evening were as bad as it gets in terms of uncertainty and fear. I noticed that my list of medications had not changed since the fever began, and other than monitoring my temperature closely, nothing else had changed. My best guess was that they knew that if I completely headed south, there was not much they could do about it. A heart can be jolted back into action. Encouraging an immune system to act when it had been eradicated by chemotherapy is another story.

The next morning, I felt horrible, but my fever was not getting any worse. Thankfully, over the next several days my body somehow fought off its enemy and some of my fear subsided.

The Business of Medicine

Soon after getting my cancer back into remission for the second time, I needed to turn my focus toward determining what treatment path I was going to take next. More chemotherapy was no longer a life-saving alternative.

I knew from my prior research that my options were limited, and my chances of survival were low. I also knew that one of those options included temporarily moving to another state so I could be treated at one of the world's best cancer clinics. I was familiar with a treatment option at the University of Minnesota, but I was compelled to hear from the best and the brightest in the world. At this point, I had to consider every option including leaving my young kids behind.

The pace of problem solving and decision making was overwhelming. I had my medical records sent across the country to the clinic that had a reputation that was second to none while I was still in the hospital, and I set up a conference call with one of their top oncologists to talk through my case shortly after being discharged. My mind was still in a haze from the chemotherapy and fever, but I had no choice but to push forward. I asked my brother to join me on the call knowing I shouldn't do it alone. The content, tone and results of that call will stick with me until I take my last breath.

Over the course of an hour, my brother and I learned about a research study that the clinic had recently launched, and a clinical trial of a cancer drug that was in the very early stages of development. We listened as the oncologist cordially talked about the study, the funding for the study, and the benefit for future cancer patients. He had almost nothing to say about me or my health.

At one point during the conversation, he commended the University of Minnesota for its work in the area, but quickly pivoted back to his sales pitch. Even through my chemo fog, I knew where this conversation was going, and I knew there was no way I was going there too.

I abruptly stopped the doctor near the end of his sales pitch and pointedly asked him, "If you were me, and your life was on the line, where would you go to get treatment? Your clinic or the University of Minnesota?" The pause on the phone line was long and uncomfortable. He was struggling.

Then the answer came: "I would go to the University of Minnesota."

The call ended shortly thereafter. My brother thanked the oncologist for his time, let him know that we were going to follow his advice, and hung up. We then sat, quietly. Our silence quickly turned into frustration, anger, and shock. A highly reputable doctor had just attempted to sell me on the idea of donating my life to fund his unproven science experiment.

I fully understand that businesses need to make money, or raise money, to be successful. In fact, over the course of my career, what has separated me from others is my ability to spot financially attractive opportunities and make money. But I am also a passionate believer that there is such a thing as a fair profit and ethical practices that need to be adhered to produce that profit.

What Is Financially Fair?

As most people realize, setting a business's corporate culture starts at the top and trickles down from there. A business's culture and associated values can be hard to define, communicate, adopt, and enforce. I think of all those things as a business's moral compass. What is right. What is clearly wrong. And what is acceptable yet in the gray area.

I mentioned earlier the well-publicized apparent missteps that Wells Fargo and EpiPen made. In those cases, a push for profits clouded sound judgment, and some challenging questions were undoubtedly presented to the leadership of both companies. I think the consensus among their customers and the business community is that these organizations had lost their way in the woods. To this day, I wonder whether the discussion my brother and I had was an isolated incident or whether that cancer clinic had drifted into the woods too.

A business owner, Jerry, once engaged me to help him sort out what proved to be an extremely complicated transition of the ownership of his company. The marketability of his business faced two significant challenges. The company had an unhealthy dependency on a small number of clients. If they lost any single client, the ongoing viability of the business would be put at risk. What's more, a plan was not in place to seamlessly transition the leadership of the company once the owner retired. Both of those things made it difficult to find an interested buyer, much less a buyer that would pay an attractive price.

Yet, because Jerry had hit a wall in terms of his desire to work, a sale of his business at some price, likely a heavily discounted price, was going to happen. To his credit, he was much more concerned with making sure his employees were happy than whether he would get more money in selling to an unknown outsider. In the end, Jerry decided to sell his business to his employees at a very attractive price.

Late one evening, Jerry and I ended up being the last two people in the building, and we got off on a tangent talking about people's true character. Until that moment, I had always seen myself as a pretty good reader of people, including whether they have a reasonably well-grounded moral compass. But Jerry had an analogy that he passed on to me that I have carried with me ever since.

"The best way to find out both an individual's and group's true character is to put a stack of money in the middle of a table and see how people decide to split it up."

I have been in situations very similar to Jerry's analogy many times since that late night discussion, and the actions and reactions are telling. Greedy people and inherently selfish people make a grab for the center of the table. Team players are willing and wanting to evenhandedly talk through why they might deserve more or less than an equal share.

Is the splitting up of a pile of money a thorough test of character? Of course not. But it sure is a good start.

I strongly suspect that the out of state oncologist my brother and I talked to was professionally and/or financially motivated to see me become one of his patients. His actions and words pointed in that direction. I often wonder what would have happened if I had not confronted him so directly. The good news is that when I deliberately asked him what was best for me, his moral compass did find true north.

Transformative lesson learned: Money can act like an aphrodisiac for some people. Seek out trusted partners who lead with honesty versus greed, as greed is an incredibly strong motivator.

CHAPTER 10

PERSEVERANCE PREVAILS

Perseverance: A Continued Effort to Achieve Something in the Face of Adversity, Failure, Opposition

I am often jealous of great business leaders who forge ahead no matter what the circumstances. While I would never label myself as a quitter, I do need to feel like something is achievable before I can fully commit to making it happen. If I can't see a path to success, I have a hard time getting started, much less reaching the desired destination. Sometimes the flaw of risk aversion has held me back when I should have kept plowing ahead.

My track record paints a picture of a hyper goal achiever. I am one. But that's because I am also a hyper goal setter. I've taken on some challenges during my life, that at first glance, looked on the edge of impossible to overcome. In most cases, the bigger the challenge, the more excited I get. Some people have asked me how I do it, and I have a simple formula for success. I consistently follow it. It works, and I would describe it as common sense.

Step #1: Set a goal
Step #2: Define a plan to get there
Step #3: Consistently track progress

Step #4: Reach the finish line
Step #5: Set another goal

The real trick is sticking to the formula and staying committed to reaching the objective. That takes tenacity, discipline, tireless effort, trial and error, and a willingness to change course when forward progress stalls. In business, goal setting is a common practice. Where I might be unusual is I have applied many aspects of goal setting to my personal life for as long as I can remember.

Honestly, I can feel a little bit lost if I am not actively pursuing a goal that I have set for myself. If I decide I want to improve my golf game, I set a goal to shoot an 83 or better. At one point in my career, I felt like I was jumping around between jobs too much. So, when I took my next job, I set a goal to remain employed with the same company for five years. My tenure at the company lasted five and a half years.

The Enormity of Cancer

Being diagnosed with cancer presented a whole new animal in terms of goal setting, action steps for success, and reaching the desired outcome. As I said previously, I love challenges. This one was a big one. Going into things, I hoped for quick success. What followed were years of adversity and unexpected setbacks. I cannot begin to tell you how much I learned about problem solving in the face of adversity along the way. My cancer diagnosis, something I would never wish upon anyone, turned into the gift that relentlessly kept giving.

After getting leukemia into remission a second time and deciding to pursue a somewhat experimental bone marrow transplant (BMT) at the University of Minnesota, the war started all over again. My second showdown with cancer was entirely different than my first. Going into my BMT, I was not in the same physical condition as when I was first diagnosed with leukemia two years prior. Not only was I getting older, but I could feel how the prior chemotherapy treatments had aged me several additional years.

Before my first battle with cancer, it took a lot to push my gas tank to empty. A year or two years into the war, I often came down with a cold or some other illness if I physically pushed things too far. While most of those minor illnesses only lasted a few days, a four-mile hike could easily force me to spend three days resting and recovering.

I checked into the hospital on August 5th, 2003, for my BMT, and the first week, prep week, consisted of receiving intense chemotherapy treatments and radiation. Within a few short days, I returned to, and surpassed, the physical low point that I had reached after five rounds of chemotherapy two years prior. I had my bone marrow transplant on August 14th.

A typical BMT transplant process is not very complicated. Unfortunately, nothing for me was typical.

The procedure starts with taking two pseudoephedrine. Some patients have an allergic reaction to the preservative that the stem cells are stored in, and the pseudoephedrine is intended to mitigate that risk. An hour later, the nurse hangs a small IV bag that contains the stem cells, and it takes about 30 minutes for them to be infused into your bloodstream. Then the waiting begins.

Over the next two weeks or more, the stem cells need to migrate to your bone marrow, engraft, grow, and start making the main components of your blood: white cells to fight infection, red cells, or hemoglobin, to distribute oxygen, and platelets which are called upon when needed to help your blood clot.

After a restless night's sleep, I swallowed two pseudoephedrine mid-morning on transplant day. But shortly after a brief celebration that my IV bag full of stem cells was dripping, I started to have severe stomach cramps. Soon, the pain was too much to take, and rather than calmly enjoying a major step forward, I was churning around on the bed in agonizing pain.

The bag of stem cells on the IV pole was soon joined by a second bag of morphine. While I remember some of what happened during the rest of that day and the next, I don't remember much. They kept me in a drug-induced haze for the better part of two days. I felt slightly better once the drugs worked their way out of my system, but not a lot.

I was told prior to my transplant that at some point during my hospital stay, I would lose my ability to eat solid food or drink anything. The radiation would temporarily damage my entire digestive tract from the top to the bottom of my body. Sure enough, on the fifth morning after my transplant, I woke up with a mild sore throat. By 5:00 p.m. that same day, I couldn't swallow. A few days later I vomited up part of the skin in my throat. So much for solid food and water for the next fifteen days.

I spent another two weeks in the hospital. During the first half of that time, I was doing what I'm sure every BMT recipient does at that stage: anxiously hoping the stem cells would successfully engraft and start working. Each day the nurses drew blood and a few hours later posted my current white cell count on the white board in my room. The number was zero for days.

Luckily, the stem cells did what they were intended to do, and the zero changed to a positive number. I could breathe a little bit. Once my new immune system kicked in, my white cell counts improved every day.

Thirty days after checking into the hospital, I checked out of the hospital. I didn't go home though. I checked into a nearby hotel room instead. I needed to stay very close to the clinic to attend daily appointments where my progress was measured closely. Those appointments took anywhere from one hour to eight hours because most days, my blood tests would indicate that I needed a transfusion of red blood cells, platelets, or both until my bone marrow could keep up with what my body needed. I once estimated that I received roughly 30 blood transfusions during the course of my disease. Thank you, Red Cross!

Because I could not drive myself to the appointments, or stay alone at the hotel, a support team of family and close friends took turns staying overnight with me and patiently attending my appointments. At this point, I was alive but barely. I remember my brother driving us back to the hotel one evening, and with ease he walked into the hotel, and up the flight of stairs toward my room on the second floor. I was winded making the very short walk from the car. I had to stop halfway up the stairs to take a breather, worried that I might pass out. He forgot what kind of shape I was in until he turned around at the top of the stairs.

I said, "This sucks" and we both started laughing.

For the first 50 days post-transplant, I took a handful of pills with breakfast, another handful at dinner, and a few more right before bed. A year or two later, it occurred to me that I had taken over 2,000 pills in the first 50 days, and most of them were so strong that I felt waves of nausea all day, every day. Throwing up daily became the norm.

While August 14th, 2003, was my physical low, March 2004 was when I really hit rock bottom. By then, my emotional gas tank was past empty and leaking too. In retrospect, I was fortunate in that I wasn't even aware of how bad things were. I stayed focused on the fact that I was alive. I was seeing my kids every day. I was done with daily blood transfusions. I guess it took me a while to realize that I was headed in the wrong direction, and that I needed to do something different.

I decided to reach out for some help.

Adding Support Team Members

The first thing I did was write a post and I placed it on the Leukemia and Lymphoma Society website. The site had a section where you could share something about your cancer story, including questions that others could see and answer. I openly wrote about how I had contracted acute leukemia which was somewhat odd for someone in their mid-30's. I shared that I'd had five rounds of chemotherapy to get the disease into remission, then relapsed, and ultimately had a bone marrow transplant. Those facts were important. But they weren't the important part of the story. I ended my post by saying that I felt alone in the war, and that I would like to hear from anyone with a similar experience, including the challenges that came with it.

The second step I took was to call my oncologist's office to ask if they were aware of any support groups that I could join. I was referred to a survivor group that they were in the process of pulling together. The participants were to be in some stage of diagnosis, treatment, and recovery from cancer, and the plan was to hold eight weekly support meetings. Caregivers or spouses were also encouraged to attend. Between the need to take care of our young kids, and likely being beyond worn out herself, my wife Christina did not accompany me to these sessions.

The meetings were intended to connect people with others that were struggling with all aspects of cancer, the organizer also shared their professional insights regarding how to best cope with the many challenges we were all facing individually, in our marriages and with our families. The get-togethers lasted two hours.

The first meeting of the small group was what you'd expect. It was a basic meet and greet including some open sharing about our disease, where we were at with treatment and recovery, and what we hoped to get from attending the seminar. Besides me, there were four other cancer patients and two spouses. One man, who looked to be in his 60s had lung cancer. I had lost my dad to lung cancer just a few years earlier, and I knew the road ahead for that couple would lead to one of them being left behind. Two of the women had breast cancer, and the other man had prostate cancer.

Our second meeting took up where we left off after the first one. We started by updating each other on what had happened since we last met. What I remember most was listening to the man with lung cancer. He had received some bad news regarding the progression of his disease, and both he and his wife were clearly having a hard time. Both women with breast cancer were past consistent treatment, but both voiced how they struggled with the nagging fear of relapse. The prostate cancer survivor was in the same place, worried about relapse.

I wasn't sure what I needed from the group, but I knew I wasn't getting it. Hearing from all of them made me feel worse, not better.

But then, as we neared the end of the second group meeting, the facilitator announced that she had homework for us. She proceeded to hand out a list of 106 items that patients often lose as a result of being diagnosed with cancer. For example, many of us had lost our hair. Some cancer patients lose their jobs. Some lose friends or even their marriage. Our takeaway was to go home and consider what we had lost, then we could look to the group for help in coping with those losses. Task master that I am, I was checking items off my list within five minutes of walking in the door of our house.

In fact, I was so focused on completing my homework that I hadn't stopped to consider how the task might affect me. I sank into a dark hole as I started checking boxes. Many boxes. Almost all of the boxes. I quickly came to realize that over the prior two and a half years I had lost almost everything on the list. Out of 106 items, I had lost 102 of them. I had left each session thinking more about everyone else's story, yet for some reason, I hadn't even considered my own circumstances. But there was my checklist, telling me it was time to face the harsh reality of my current situation rather than deny it existed.

At the next meeting, we started by sharing what we learned starting with the gentlemen next to me with lung cancer. He had lost 73 things. Each of the two women with breast cancer had lost 50-something items on their lists, and the man with prostate cancer 40-something. By the time they came around to me, any remaining shred of denial was stripped away. I shared my number, there were a few minutes of silence, and then I distinctly remember the following comments made by two of the patients.

"Honestly, I am surprised you have the energy to be here."

"When I see you, I feel overwhelmed as I don't know where to begin to help you."

At that moment, I knew I had a lot of challenges to work through if I was going to reach my goal of beating cancer. I had reached out for help, hoping I would find others who were experiencing the same things that I was. In some ways, I had found that. But in some ways, I felt more alone than ever.

Filling Team Gaps

Hitting rock bottom had an emotional impact on me like none other. I knew I had no choice but to fight forward. But I also knew that the support group meetings would end in a few short weeks, and I would be left on an island to fight alone.

Then nothing short of a miracle happened.

After sharing my long list of losses with my support group, I returned home to an unread email. My post left on the Leukemia and Lymphoma Society site had been answered.

> Reply to your email - Leukemia & Lymphoma Society
> 4/28/2004
>
> Hi Kevin,
>
> I have only just started going on the internet and looking through websites about leukemia and lymphoma. I had a bone marrow transplant from an unrelated donor on July 03 aged 31. I was first diagnosed with AML in August 2001 and was in remission until April 2003. I go for checkups every two weeks, and I am doing very well just trying to get off the medication now and I will feel great. I recently took a reiki healing course that I practice on myself, and this has made a huge difference to the healing process. Good luck with your journey to lead a normal life and I send healing thoughts your way.
>
> Kind Regards
>
> Justine

I had found someone else on my empty island.

Justine lived in London, which happens to be one of my favorite travel destinations in the world, and over the next few days, we exchanged a handful of lengthy emails. As her email states, she was diagnosed with the same form of leukemia that I had. Her diagnosis happened within days of the same month and year of when I was diagnosed. She had five rounds of chemotherapy, achieved remission, relapsed, then had a bone marrow transplant just like I had. Those things all happened within weeks of when they happened to me.

A few lengthy emails turned into months of daily emails. We both had others around us who cared about us deeply, but something was missing. There were times that exchanging emails wasn't enough, so Justine and I called each other instead. When I said a miracle happened, I did not say it lightly. Justine filled a hole in my support team that nobody else could fill. I hope I did half as much for her. Collectively, we both beat cancer.

When Justine and I were both well down the road to recovery, I flew to London, and we met face to face. The emails and phone calls were great. Seeing her in person and celebrating that we had both survived, brought a whole new level of personal connection for me.

Transformative lesson learned: When your challenges at work or at home seem insurmountable, hope, and pray for a miracle. You might just get one.

CHAPTER 11

WIN/WIN OR WIN/LOSE

Reacting Out of Anger is Tempting, but Anger Often Clouds the Road to Success

Two years after my second trip down the road with leukemia, I started feeling like I had found some solid ground to stand on. I still had a sometimes-paralyzing fear of a second relapse, but I learned to cope with that fear as best I could. Then I began noticing my left hip was giving me some troubles. At first, it was just a minor annoyance that would appear after taking a long walk or hike. Then, in an instant, during a vacation in New York City, it went from minor discomfort to a serious problem.

I was stepping out of a cab when I felt a crunch in my hip joint. It wasn't particularly painful, but I immediately knew that something wasn't right. Back home, my family doctor reminded me that problems with bones and joints are a very common long-term side effect for BMT patients. I am sure the first time I heard about those long-term possibilities, my mind was busy trying to process what was right in front of me instead. My general practitioner referred me to an orthopedic surgeon which should have been a clue as to what was coming.

During my first appointment with the surgeon, I learned that my left hip joint had avascular necrosis, the death of bone tissue due to a lack of blood supply. The ball that was nestled into the socket of my joint, had cracked when I stepped out of the cab. For months after my transplant, I had taken large doses of steroids to ward off rejection of my new immune system. As is the case for many successful cancer treatments, those steroids had solved one problem while creating a new, more manageable one.

During that appointment I also learned that over time, my pain was destined to get worse, not better, so a total hip replacement was a matter of when, not if. But none of it was urgent. Given that I already had some of the classic symptoms of Post-Traumatic Stress Disorder (PTSD) from everything else I had been through, I really wanted to put surgery and another hospital stay off for as long as I could.

My reprieve did not last long though. Within a few short months, I was finding it difficult to walk three blocks. Worse, I could no longer get a decent night's rest as every time I rolled over in bed the pain woke me up. As much as I was trying to escape being stuck in a hospital jail cell again, I didn't have much of a choice. I reluctantly scheduled the surgery. Thankfully I did because the pain rapidly progressed.

As usual, I did my research to find a doctor that I could put my faith in to perform my hip replacement. The surgeon I chose had performed one of the first minimally invasive hip replacements in the state of Minnesota. He was well known and very highly respected. As he and I spoke, it was clear that he wasn't just a very smart guy. I could tell that he cared about his patients too. Plus, he had assembled a talented, thoughtful team around him. His assistant took care of every detail which was a big plus. After several painful days and nights, the date of surgery arrived.

An Easy Surgery Goes Sideways

Once again, I checked into a hospital. Less than five steps into the front door, I felt the familiar scent of hospital soap and hand sanitizer hit my nose. Ten steps in, and I was reminded of the intense fear and memories of my previous hospital stays. Intellectually I knew this time was different. But rational thoughts do not always override irrational fear. I held onto the thought that this was supposed to be an easy surgery. Ironically, a total hip replacement now sounded easy to me.

Within hours of checking in, I was put under, and the surgery started. I was very thankful I would be out cold for a few hours of my stay. And I really didn't care about how much pain I would experience right after surgery or as part of rehab and recovery in the days and weeks that followed. I was used to being in pain. I only cared about getting out of the hospital as soon as I could.

When I came to, however, I awoke to some rather troubling news. While they were doing their work, a surgical measuring device- think of a ball about the size of a large marble- came loose, and they couldn't find it given the minimally invasive incision. The surgeon was pretty sure he knew where it had migrated to, but they needed to be sure. They stopped the procedure, gave me an additional dose of anesthesia to put me under further, wheeled me to X-ray, and confirmed what had happened.

The ball had migrated from the outside of my hip, around the bottom of my pelvis, to my groin, where it could not be easily retrieved. The team had no choice but to finish the hip replacement and leave the sizing ball in its new home.

Anger or Acceptance

When they broke the news to me two hours after surgery, I was still in a groggy fog. My wife was angry. I was numb. The surgeon was aware of my prior health history, and he was visibly shaken trying to explain what happened. He told me that it was possible that the ball could be left in its current location for months or even years. Or, he said he could put me under again in a day or two, make an incision near my pubic bone, and fish out the ball from there. Another surgery and hospital stay could not have been less appealing. I told him I needed to think about it overnight.

The next morning, I was exhausted, still nauseous from the anesthesia, and in pain from the hip replacement. I am pretty sure the second dose of the anesthesia didn't do me any favors. My wife called me at the crack of dawn, emotionally ragged and overwhelmed. Out of anger and frustration, she broached the subject of taking legal action against the doctor and the hospital. While I could totally appreciate her anger, I was a lot closer to acceptance. And why would I go there anyway? I knew that there was no amount of money that could change the fact that between this most recent surgery setback and my diagnosis with cancer and treatment, I had been raped of any sense of security regarding my health.

A couple of hours after that early morning phone call, I was predictably the first stop for the surgeon. After the usual greetings and check-in regarding how the hip felt, I told him that I wanted to take a wait-and-see approach to a second surgery. I also assured him that I did not blame him for anything. Mistakes happen. I was not going to be mad or hold a grudge toward him. The relief on his face when he heard my words was immediate.

He proceeded to tell me that he hadn't slept the night before. He had replayed every step of the surgery over and over in his mind, and he still wasn't sure how it happened. His words were sincere, and unrehearsed. During that moment, I think we were both smart enough to know that his medical malpractice insurance would cover any financial claim I pursued. And my health insurance would cover any further medical costs. Once money, anger, and blame were put aside, we could both focus on acceptance. More importantly for me, I could turn my entire attention to getting healthy and out of the hospital.

The Uncertainty of Legal Claims

Very early in my career, I worked with a brilliant investment banker who told me a story about a financial transaction that he worked on that ultimately went sideways. The deal made its way through the legal system until the day when the facts and circumstances were to be presented to a judge. Both sides of the transaction appeared in court after spending months preparing to argue their position, each leaning on specific language in the financial and legal documents that supported their respective cases.

The hearing started just as everyone expected, with the judge telling both parties that he had thoroughly read and reviewed the contracts and supporting documentation. But then, he held up a large legal file and set it aside. He apparently wasn't interested in what the investment bankers, attorneys, and clients had spent hours drafting and redrafting.

The judge then said that while he appreciated what the documentation tried to spell out, like most adversarial situations, even the best bankers and lawyers could not accurately predict and capture in words an entire set of facts and circumstances. He then asked both parties to verbally summarize what they intended the deal to be. It seems he wanted to help everyone find a more swift and efficient way forward.

The judge in this case was highly regarded for his long tenure and extensive experience practicing the law. During the verbal arguments, it became clear that he had some very understandable weaknesses in his financial skills. He was a judge, not a financier. Financial transactions can be very complicated, analytically technical, and filled with nuance. Rather than spend hours educating himself on the specifics of the transaction, he chose to focus on what he is charged to do: solve disputes.

My colleague went into the courtroom almost certain that he and his client would prevail. He left the courtroom aghast by how a decision was rendered based on a somewhat brief verbal summary of facts and circumstances rather than a full understanding of the analytically complicated transaction.

Ever since I heard that story, I have tried to steer clear of business and personal dealings that have even a remote possibility of ending up in front of a judge. You never know what the outcome will be. The time commitment, anger, and negative energy of the fight can be draining too. I have found that the best way to avoid legal disagreements is to focus on building relationships with honorable people whose intentions are noble and clear.

Earlier in this book I relayed an experience where I had worked with a less than honorable real estate developer in Charlotte. There were many opportunities to bring legal action against the parties, and it would have been very easy to get angry and confrontational. But I knew that process would be fraught with uncertainty. Not to mention that the time, energy, and legal fees required to pursue a claim would have been a sunk cost. Our consistent, and I feel, appropriate, decision was to mitigate our exposure outside of a courtroom.

Acceptance Has Rewards

Setting aside one's frustration or anger by taking a long-term perspective is not always easy, but I have found it generally pays off. For example, should I have brought a claim against my well-intentioned surgeon? Or was I better off to forgo the emotional turmoil and a potential financial settlement? I know the answer to those questions. But you may have some doubts.

Three years later, I began to have some unusual pain in my groin. Through the process of assessing what was causing my pain, the medical team wanted to eliminate prostate cancer as an option. Ultimately the surgical ball turned out to be the problem, but the prostate screening came back positive for early-stage prostate cancer.

The medical equipment, my prostate, and the prostate cancer were removed during a single surgery. Once again, I had to endure the smell of hospital soap, sanitizer, and the traumatic memories that they trigger. But luckily, I didn't need any chemotherapy or radiation this time around.

I can only imagine what would have happened if I had immediately pursued a medical claim against my well-respected surgeon rather than taking a wait-and-see approach. I am almost certain the medical ball would have been surgically removed sooner to mitigate any further risk of its presence. A prostate screening would have never been performed giving the prostate cancer cells ample amount of time to quietly multiply and spread.

There isn't a day that goes by that I am not thankful that I made the right decision. Alternatively, I could have won a heated confrontation in a courtroom and ultimately lost my life to prostate cancer. That feels a lot like a win/lose outcome to me.

Transformative lesson learned: Legal cases are uncertain, steeped in anger, and the chances of winning are unfavorable. I prefer the near 100% success rate of collaborating with the right trusted partners instead.

CHAPTER 12

BREAKUPS ARE PART OF LIFE

Finding a Winning Formula Under Trying Circumstances

While I can't claim that this was my grand plan from the start, my career path has largely followed my need for variety and my interest in accumulating a very broad array of skills and experiences. I was successfully managing over $1 billion of assets by my early thirties which gave me the opportunity to compare notes with the managing partner of Goldman Sachs in his New York office. A few years later, I bought a manufacturing company with my brother and became proficient at operating a forklift. My breadth of skills and interests have always served me well working with small companies.

That doesn't mean my skills have always been a perfect fit for each new client. Sometimes, I've needed to be a quick study. Other times, it's been a tedious learning curve that I have struggled to get through. Every client and every business are different, and that can be new and exciting, or at times, overwhelming.

A few years ago, I was presented with an opportunity to partner with a group of others to acquire a business. The company was right in my sweet spot. It had twenty-five employees, which was big enough to have some mass, but small enough that I felt confident that my abilities would be valuable from the get-go. The business had suffered inconsistent profitability, and it was also missing some critical infrastructure, including a few gaping holes in the leadership team. One of their most urgent issues was a need for someone to be accountable for generating revenue. The business's inconsistent profitability was a symptom of hoping new revenue would land without a well thought out process to capture it.

What made me most excited about the opportunity was the fact that of the four soon-to-be owners, I felt like I had the most experience operating and managing all aspects of a small company. My three partners excelled in other critical areas of the business, and they had valuable long-standing business relationships within its market. I lacked both of those things. The complementary skills of the team sounded like an attractive combination where I could focus on things I knew well, and my partners could do the same.

Regrettably, once the deal closed it soon became apparent that my partners and I weren't going to be on the same page. It takes a wide breadth of skills to efficiently manage an entrepreneurial company, and time-sensitive decisions often languished due to their lack of small company experience. To make matters worse, each of them voiced discomfort with delegating those decisions to any of the other members of the partner group. At first, I found this paralysis confusing. Where was this inability to move forward coming from? But as time went on, the root cause became increasingly apparent.

We didn't trust each other.

Business Partnership Mismatch

At the beginning of our partnership, a lack of trust was understandable. We were in the Introduction Stage of relationship development that I described in more detail in Chapter 8. All of us were happy and our meetings were filled with hope and promise. Our partnership sailed through the Dating Stage, even as some cracks in our foundation of trust had started to appear. We avoided hard, or uncomfortable discussions, and as a result, decisions were often avoided. By the time we arrived at Stage 3, Differences & Compromise, the growth of our relationship had come to a halt.

Here is what that distrust looked like.

During one of several individual discussions with one of my partners, we openly discussed the fact that the group struggled to make timely decisions. I suggested something that seemed to me to be a painless solution. I proposed that we appoint a leader, or a "managing partner," as management by committee has some well-known flaws. If the leader we appointed consistently made decisions that the remaining partners didn't like, the managing partner could be removed at any time. That conversation ended with the comment, "I have worked for several different companies, and I have never worked for a president who I thought did a good job." Consider the trust warning signs embedded in that comment.

Soon, that mistrust permeated everything, even our year-end process for reviewing employee performance. The partners all knew how important it was to review and openly discuss individual performance with each employee. But over the course of several meetings, we explored a long list of options for implementing a review process for each partner and couldn't agree on a solution. One of my partners captured the fears and mistrust that we were suffering from perfectly when she said, "I feel like something could be said during the review process that the partner being reviewed will never recover from."

One of the key reasons I joined the company was to become part of a highly functioning team that ultimately achieves remarkable results. I believed then, and continue to believe now, that a highly functioning team is one made up of people who can seamlessly work together and trust each other in a similar way as they trust their best friend or spouse. I took it for granted that my partners would value working relationships in the same way that I did.

The partners' inability to trust each other reared its head many times. Despite our superior individual skills and shared desire to reach our true potential, our team chemistry slowly eroded. I lost confidence that we could ultimately come together to produce the kind of success I had hoped for. And I was able to pinpoint why: my partners were very comfortable with group decision-making and, therefore less risky, group accountability. I preferred to grant an individual the responsibility to make decisions and then hold that same person accountable for their results.

There were no bad people. Just four talented partners who believed in different ways to trust, delegate, and reward.

Once that became clear to me, my next step also became clear. It was time for us to part ways. I needed to pursue an alternative opportunity where I could surround myself with others who found value in the same things that I do.

Rather than abruptly resign, I spent the next several months thoughtfully working with my partners to agree on the specifics and timing of the transition of my duties and ultimately my exit. I was committed to doing what was right for all parties to ensure the best outcome for the team and each of its members.

After very carefully charting out that course of action, my ownership was paid off. I left the business knowing that my partners and I had done everything we could to leave the company in a better place than when we bought it. That fact was validated by the company's sale to a strategic buyer within a couple of months of my departure with a very attractive ROI for all of us.

Personal Relationship Mismatch

Anyone who has been through a life-altering experience like a cancer diagnosis will be the first to admit that those types of tests are very hard on a marriage. If there were small cracks in the relationship prior to the event, those cracks can turn into the Grand Canyon in the months and years that follow.

Shortly before being diagnosed with cancer, I was in a horrible spot in my marriage. My wife and I were not getting along, and I felt like our differences were starting to outnumber our similarities. Christina grew up in a family where her dad, a teacher, held the same job for decades and he was the main breadwinner in the family. She thrived in an environment of consistency and stability. The only consistent thing that I gravitated toward was change.

Back then, and still today, I had an insatiable hunger for continuous learning. I also had a high tolerance for risk and a deep-seated need to experience and explore the world around me. Thankfully, I proved to myself that I was very good at finding a way to make money, no matter what choices I made in my career. By the time I was thirty years old, I was in a very lucrative job and on a clear path to retiring within a few years if I remained at that job. Rather than follow the safe road, I resigned and started my first business.

That is the lifestyle that I am drawn to. I most enjoyed career moves that kept me challenged, and my monthly paycheck did not have the same consistency of a long tenured teacher. It's a way of living that works for me, but it's not for everyone.

As our marriage matured, Christina's interests and needs became almost polar opposite to mine. She put a high priority on a close-knit family, and most nights, she was content watching TV or reading a good book. She craved predictability. Naturally, my thirst for change and frequent career moves threatened her sense of security. But we both had young children that meant the world to us. We wanted to make our marriage last.

Years passed, and we slowly watched each other turn into someone who no longer shared our dreams. She dreamed of spending quiet nights at home with our kids. I dreamed of taking our kids on adventuresome escapes to New York City, Paris, or the Swiss Alps.

After several years, I was at a crossroads. I knew we both wanted to make our marriage work, but we weren't even in sync on how to get the help our marriage needed. I couldn't face staying in such an unfulfilling marriage and I couldn't digest the prospect of getting a divorce, as I knew a divorce would create long lasting emotional baggage for our kids. That is when a third option began to slowly creep into my thoughts. With no good alternatives in sight, my last option was to give up on life. When I received the news that I had cancer in my bone marrow, the core of me, I was not surprised.

The first several days of my initial hospital stay became a period of soul searching. Someone or something had sent me a clear message that I had to stop in my tracks and deal with my disease. And that disease was not leukemia. I made a conscious choice to fight to survive knowing that my personal survival would most likely lead to the end of my marriage. I countered that depressing thought with the dream that someday I would find a partner who would be willing to live their life at the same pace that I did.

Six years after my first diagnosis, and once my survival was no longer in question, I knew the time had come to address a long simmering problem. It felt like I was taking another step backward rather than forward. Ending a long-term marriage is painful no matter what the circumstances are. In my case, cancer was a trip through hell and back for my kids, and I needed to give very careful consideration to what the ending of their parents' marriage would do to them.

I also wanted to give very careful consideration to what Christina had lived through. I knew I had been disengaged as a marriage partner while fighting for my life, leaving her as a single parent raising our three kids. Cancer was cruel to our whole family. It was important to me that we all individually survived intact rather than broken. Our marriage ended as one more casualty of my diagnosis.

Shortly after our divorce was finalized, Christina found another man to add to her life. Both of us put a very high priority on the wellbeing of our kids before my diagnosis, and that commitment remained through our separation, divorce, and still today. Like any divorced couple, we have had some differences, but we have always found a way to productively work through them. That has been rewarding for me and hopefully rewarding for her too.

The success of our kids has been the product of their own perseverance, coupled with the support of two parents committed to them no matter what the circumstances. They each had the courage and resolve to attend college in another state, and graduate in four years. They have a long life in front of them and I feel confident in their prospects.

A counselor once told me that I needed a racecar and a fully engaged woman sitting next to me in it to be happy. He was right. I absolutely found that woman in my current wife, Gretchen. We were married fourteen years after my diagnosis. Cross off #3 on my list of items lost due to cancer!

Transformative lesson learned: Sometimes a personal or professional partnership doesn't work because it never will. Yet with hard work up until and through the end of the relationship, a win/win outcome can be achieved.

CHAPTER 13

URGENCY VS REGRET

When Cancer Knocked on My Door, I Ignored It. My Neighbor Opened the Door Instead

I should give you a heads-up that this chapter is chronologically out of order. I chose to put this chapter very close to the end of my book because I think it is the most powerful experience I had during the period I was entangled with cancer.

What follows changed my life. It changed my perspective on how I live my life. In writing the previous chapters, it brought back memories that at times, are hard to relive. If I could pay one thing forward to help others, that message is in this chapter.

But first, let me spell out the chronology of my adventure. I was first diagnosed with leukemia in late July of 2001. My cancer returned in May of 2003, and I had a bone marrow transplant in August of that same year. I was in the hospital for thirty days for the transplant, then released from the hospital to live in an apartment nearby. When I left the hospital at the end of those thirty days, I felt drained and barely alive, yet cautiously optimistic that I was moving forward rather than backward.

But eighteen days later I took a U-turn and had to check back into the hospital.

It is actually somewhat expected for a BMT recipient to experience some level of rejection from their new immune system. Symptoms of rejection are many as it can affect joints, digestion, eyes, muscles, skin, blood cell counts, etc. Rejection is one of the main causes of death in the days and weeks after transplant. In my case, I had a small skin rash while I was in the hospital, and that rash then spread to most of my body after I moved into the hotel. The plan was to put me back into the hospital for seven days, give me a strong dose of drugs by IV, and get the rejection under control.

My return trip to the hospital was a little bit different than my thirty days stay for the transplant in that I did not need to be confined to my proverbial jail cell. My immune system, although weak, was working, and I regularly roamed the halls or made meals in the kitchenette. I also got to know some of the people who were consistently at the hospital in support of patients who were in different stages of transplantation and recovery.

One evening, while sitting in the visitor's lounge, I struck up a conversation with a mother and father anxiously monitoring the progress of their 20-year-old son. The longer we spoke, the more we found in common.

Like me, their son had been diagnosed with a disease that required a bone marrow transplant. Like me, he was suffering complications. I even learned that he and I had received our transplants on the same day. But that's where our similarities diverged. His complications were severe and stubborn. Mine seemed to be dissipating with my treatment. I had been lucky enough to leave the hospital for eighteen days. He was still in the same room that he'd checked into fifty days earlier.

His parents shared with me that the stem cells he had been given on his transplant day had failed to engraft, leaving him without a functioning immune system. One problem had been followed by another one, and an infection had recently developed in his lungs. Throughout our conversations, his parents voiced their optimism that the doctors had a plan of attack. I so wanted to believe their optimism, but I knew their son's chances of survival were slim. Yes, I felt a twinge of relief that I wasn't experiencing what he was, and that I was likely to return to my house and kids one day soon. But I also couldn't help but feel the anxiety, uncertainty, stress, and sadness that the patient and family were suffering through too.

The next day I ran into the patient's mother and father again in the visitor lounge. Their tiny shred of optimism was fraying. Their son had taken a turn for the worse. Things had disintegrated so quickly that his doctors were not even sure what specifically had gone wrong, but his health was failing at a rate they could not manage. Later that day, the bad news was delivered. The doctors had lost hope. The mother and father had been told that their son would not live through the night.

The young man's time was ending after less than twenty years of life. I fought to understand why it wasn't me instead.

Because his room was right next to mine, I could hear crying through our shared hospital wall. As the day turned into evening, I started to hear more voices right outside of my door, as his family and friends began to gather. At first, there were just a few voices. Soon I could hear many. I reluctantly opened my door, unsure whether I could emotionally handle what I might see.

The entire wing of the hospital was filled with approximately one hundred 20-year-old faces, sitting on the floor, trying to cope with what would inevitably happen. His extended family stayed huddled in the visitors lounge nearby. The memory of opening that door and seeing those kids will never escape me.

My nurse was visibly shaken when she stopped in to check on me. "Days like this must be incredibly hard for you," I said quietly.

She agreed, "It is so hard to get to know patients on this floor because not all of you are going to make it."

Her job seemed impossible. Yet, without her and others like her, my war with cancer would have been impossible. I said, "I couldn't do your job."

She replied, "It is because of people like you. Those that will make it. That is why we are all here."

As the night wore on, I could hear the patient in the room next door struggling in his bed through our shared wall. I knew a young man was fighting a losing battle to survive. At 3:00 a.m., I opened the door of my room to a sea of mostly young faces crying, holding each other, or silent in sadness. I ran into the young man's father right outside of my room, and we both lost our emotional composure when we embraced.

His son's life ended a few minutes later.

Fear of Taking Action

To this day, when I hear someone say the words "Someday I will……." I cringe. I want to tell them about this young man. I want to grab them by the shoulders, shake them, and say, "What if you don't get to your someday? What are you waiting for?"

I spent way too much time in my earlier life living under the common but utterly ridiculous assumption that life lasts forever. Intellectually, I have always known it doesn't. So have you.

So why does it take a catastrophic event to make us fully grasp reality? My gift from being diagnosed with cancer is that I get it now. I fearlessly take actions based on the reality that life is short rather than complacently knowing the certainty of death without acting.

To be clear, I am not just talking about taking that dream vacation or calling it quits in a bad romance. Acting with urgency applies to the thousands of hours we spend every year working too. Decisions that business leaders make everyday impact others in the same way that parents' decisions impact their kids' lives.

Honestly, I am surprised by the number of companies that consistently lose sight of the advice first shared by Benjamin Franklin: "Remember that time is money." Decisions that aren't made in a timely fashion or actions that are pushed off until a later date are expensive. Likewise, decisions made in haste or fear are equally damaging. The costs aren't just financial either. Employee trust and goodwill can be damaged too. Whenever an executive takes a leadership position in a business, they are granted the opportunity, privilege, and the burden of making tough decisions for the good of the people around them.

A few years ago, I did some work for a company that was faced with one of those hard decisions. The business had unexpectedly lost one of its larger clients. With that loss came numerous challenges, the hardest of which was the uncomfortable fact that 100% of one employee's job had been dedicated to servicing the lost client. She was a very talented woman with extremely marketable skills. But those skills were not a good fit for the remaining client base.

Over the next several months, the company's leadership meticulously explored and rehashed their options. I watched in amazement as several weeks in, no decisive action was taken. Instead, a "decision" based largely on deep conflict avoidance was made to task the employee's manager to find other work for the employee. It was painfully apparent that her skills did not fit any other work.

Time continued to move forward. Once it became clear that trying to fit a round peg into a square hole wasn't going to work, the team moved onto its next "decision": hope the employee would figure it out on their own and resign. Firing a nice person was too much to digest. Respecting the employee with the conversation that she deserved was, apparently, not worth the leadership team's personal discomfort.

Even more frustrating for me: Shortly after the client was lost, I advised the leadership team to take a specific and doable set of steps that would have saved everyone so much heartache and loss. Here is the simple roadmap I walked the team through:

1. Start with an open discussion with the employee.
2. Tell the truth and explain the facts and circumstances.
3. Explain to the employee that they are valued, leadership felt horrible, and that the goal was to find a solution that was best for all parties.
4. Further explain that all reasonable options have been explored and that the employee transitioning away from the company is in everyone's best interest.
5. Come to an agreement as to when that transition will take place, and then create reasonable space and time for it to happen.

I don't believe in abruptly firing anyone unless there is cause, so I suggested that a 90-day transition period was very reasonable.

During that three-month time period, the employee needed to actively look for a new position while getting paid by the company. But at the end of 90 days, both parties would part ways. As with most terminations of employment, there were additional items to consider including digital security, but all those details could be addressed. I was highly confident the employee would find a new home within that allotted time due to her attractive skillset.

Weeks went by, with everyone suffering under the weight of the obvious problem, and the employee swirled in the false hope that a new job at the company would somehow materialize. Finally, the conversation was tackled. Everyone felt immediate relief. The employee launched a very effective job search and landed a higher paying, more personally satisfying job well within the three-month transition period.

The Tangled Web of Indecision

Take a minute and consider how this example of leadership indecision affected the other employees at the company, and the owners of the business too. The money spent paying the salary and benefits for a job that no longer existed resulted in lower profitability. That in turn impacted the annual amount contributed to the employee profit sharing plan. Worse yet, the morale and productivity of everyone around the misplaced employee was affected too. It was all a waste.

I ran into the employee six months later, and she couldn't have been happier. She gave me every impression that the long period of indecision had been bad for her too. She should have moved sooner. It was leadership's responsibility to lead the way forward, and they sat still instead.

So why is this chapter the last one? Within a few short hours after I checked into the hospital for the very first time after being diagnosed with cancer, I posed the following question to myself: Did I regret any choices I had made in my life? After an hour or two of thinking about it, without hesitation I landed on the answer. No. With the certainty of that answer, I could easily turn my attention to tackling the challenges that lie ahead instead of wallowing in the regret of what I may have missed in my life.

Living a life of urgency at home and in the office can seem risky at times. It is risky. But when we let fear get in the way of what is important and urgent, the result is regret. Which would you prefer just prior to taking your last breath? A life filled with risk, success, and sometimes failure? Or a life filled with regret because you always hoped your someday would arrive?

Transformative lesson learned: Turn your personal and professional somedays into today.

CHAPTER 14

CONCLUSION

I had two specific goals in writing this book.

For starters, my children were very young when cancer entered their lives, and they have heard many of the stories that are written here already. Their memories will fade just like mine, and this book will serve as a timeless reminder for them to turn off their computers and cell phones and pay attention to the people right in front of them instead. In particular, their dad!

I am also personally troubled by our increasing reliance on social media and digital communication tools to develop, maintain, and manage relationships with significant others, friends, customers, employees, and vendors. I intend to share my story with as many people as I can to encourage them to develop more intimate, and productive relationships as a means to live a more meaningful and successful life.

I have come to realize that I will need to put a checkmark next to each of the following items to feel as though I have lived this life to the fullest.

- **Career:** I think most people would be happy to exchange places with me in terms of what I have accomplished during my career.

- **Children:** The day that I was diagnosed with leukemia was the day I moved my three kids to #1 on my priority list. That decision has paid invaluable dividends.

- **Marriage:** My marriage failed the first time around, which I still regret today. But the second time I got it right for sure!

- **Giving Back:** While I have tried to help others as much as I can over the years, I know I need to do more. Writing this book and sharing its content with others is my attempt to do more.

I recognize that I could have written a personal book about the trials that I faced with my cancer diagnosis, survival, and recovery. Alternatively, I could have written a business book about the many challenges and successes I have had in my business career. I decided to attempt to climb a more difficult mountain by showing readers how I have combined my work life with my personal life to achieve success and a more meaningful outcome.

Whether by choice or unfortunate circumstances, I have never taken the easy route. It's been a fantastic journey so far. I hope you have enjoyed reading some of the highlights.

ABOUT KEVIN JANSEN

Kevin is an accomplished entrepreneur and business consultant, father, spouse, world traveler, and cancer survivor. He rarely sits still, and when he is faced with upcoming free time, it's quickly filled with an excursion to New York City, London, the Swiss Alps, or to where his three adult children now live.

In the middle of his successful career, Kevin was diagnosed with acute myeloid leukemia (AML), an aggressive and often fatal form of cancer. Physically and emotionally surviving from that diagnosis is the crown jewel of his resume.

Learn more at: www.mayhillconsulting.com.

www.ingramcontent.com/pod-product-compliance
Lightning Source LLC
LaVergne TN
LVHW041339080426
835512LV00006B/531